BEYOND THE LIGHT

by
Diane Marshall

authorHOUSE®

AuthorHouse™ UK Ltd.
500 Avebury Boulevard
Central Milton Keynes, MK9 2BE
www.authorhouse.co.uk
Phone: 08001974150

First published by AuthorHouse 1/15/2008

ISBN: 978-1-4343-3466-4 (sc)

Printed in the United States of America
Bloomington, Indiana

This book is printed on acid-free paper.

ACKNOWLEDGEMENTS

———◆———

This book would not have been written without the love and encouragement of my wonderful family. Thanks to my husband John for his enduring support. To my son Mark and my daughter Tracey, who never gave up on me. Being your mother is the greatest of honours and I love you guys. I am blessed with so many special friends who bring a light into my life and I thank you all. Carol, Gerry, Jim, Liz, Helen, Alistair, Alison, Irene, Helen, Colin, Emma and Keith and my daughter in-laws Alison and Sharon – thanks guys. And for those I don't have room to mention, but you know who you are.

There are times in our lives when we have the privilege of knowing special people and this is for Jimmy who died before completion of this book:

God bless you my friend, you taught me the meaning of humility. See you later.

'For I know the plans I have for you, declares the Lord, plans to prosper you and not to harm you, plans to give you hope and a future.'
Jeremiah 29 V. 11

Grateful thanks to Duncan Brown for creating the beautiful painting for the front of my book, an amazing artist, friend and a gentleman.
Artist Duncan Brown
www.handpict.org.uk

Author's Note

Good and evil surround us from the moment we enter this world, but during the process of birth we lose the wisdom of our souls. Sometimes the path of evil is the only one that awakens us to our true essence, and sometimes, it's too late!

Beyond the light is a work of fiction and is not intended to give true accounts of near death experience.

CHAPTER ONE

The police car escorted the ambulance at high speed through the streets of the city with lights flashing and sirens blasting. The clouds that had been a mere threat earlier burst like overfilled balloons, sending torrents of rain crashing down onto the crowded streets below. In the back of the ambulance two paramedics anxiously fought to save the life of the woman they had dragged clear of the tangled mess that was once her car. Behind them in close pursuit followed Gerry Brookes and his four year old daughter Alison in a sky blue Mercedes. His white-knuckled grip on the steering wheel made it difficult to manoeuvre the car on the wet slippery road. He glanced into the rear view mirror at his daughter whose tear stained face was pale, and a worried expression creased her brow. "Mummy's going to be all right sweetheart," he assured her, silently praying to God that he was right. But the child was not listening – she was busy watching the winged creatures flying through the darkening sky. When the ambulance finally stopped outside the accident and emergency entrance, Gerry sprang out of his car like a frightened gazelle and ran to the side of his wife's stretcher. A young man dressed in white tunic and trousers appeared by his side as the medical crew rushed the injured woman inside.

"Please wait for just a moment." said the medic whose face was full of concern as he regarded this man who looked to be near a state of collapse himself. "My name is Mark Barnes," said the young man "and I'm one of the A&E nurses; best get you inside out of this weather."

"I have to see my wife." said Gerry, his voice breaking…

"Let them get on with assessing the situation so that they can deal with it without delay sir, but first we have to get a few details…"

"Details, what? My wife is dying in there." Alison was now sitting in the back of a police car and the young female officer had been asking her about her nursery but the child's thoughts were elsewhere.

"I want to see my daddy now." she said as she withdrew her hand from the constable's grip and scrambled out of the car. As she ran the short distance across the windswept parking area the icy rain stung her legs and face. When she reached Gerry she tugged on the bottom of his jacket and cried, "Daddy, mummy's going to get better; the big angel that went into the hospital with her will take care of her."

"What did you say"? Gerry asked.

The young male nurse was intent on getting them into the waiting room and took Alison by the hand. "Come along we'll take daddy inside shall we?" he suggested, as he guided them through a door and into a small room that looked nothing like a hospital waiting room. Gerry followed behind them feeling as though he was sleepwalking. Looking around the room, he felt physically sick. It was too much like a lounge in a well kept home, complete with a television that had a large selection of DVDs, music system, large sofas, beautifully arranged flowers, and a large window that was tastefully dressed with subtly patterned drapes looking out onto a small gardened area to the rear of the hospital. The coffee table had assorted books sitting on top of it. There was even an en-suite, complete with all the requisite accessories, and there was no sound or smell of the bustling hospital outside the door. The only thing out of place was the typical hospital tray with white cups and saucers sitting on top of a small unit with tea and coffee making facilities, and individually wrapped biscuits. Gerry stood in the middle of the room whilst Alison flicked through the selection of DVDs.

"So this is the bad news room is it?" said Gerry "Very nice, very nice indeed, oh of course it's meant to soften the blow is that it?"

Alison started to cry, bringing Gerry out of his despair, and he sat down beside her on the sofa and pulled her onto his lap.

"I'm sorry sweetheart; daddy didn't mean what he said just now, everything is going to be all right." He looked up at the medic "I'm sorry; you see I couldn't bear to lose her."

"I can see that" he said "Look, I'm going to see how she's doing and I'll let you know as soon as I can, but in the meantime, I'll send someone in to get your wife's details okay?"

Gerry nodded, and tried to control his rising panic.

"You'll find the nurses station just at the end the hall if you need anything and you will be kept in the picture at all times; my name is Mark so if you need me just shout…"Just then his pager bleeped. He hastily moved toward the door, and as he opened it Gerry's parents rushed in to comfort their son and granddaughter.

Once Mark had closed the door on the tormented family he stood there for a few moments feeling totally helpless and heart sorry for the family. "Sometimes, I hate this fucking job." he muttered under his breath as he walked away. Mia's face had turned ashen and the medical team were trying frantically to keep her alive.

"We've lost her!" shouted one doctor, whose face looked tired and strained as he studied his patient closely. Mia could hear every word as she lay there motionless and without a heartbeat. Suddenly she found herself floating above all the commotion. She could see herself lying there with tubes in her arms, and she watched as they prepared to shock her back to life. She felt confused, and wondered why they were all running around, for she felt warm, loved and safe. From somewhere behind her, the ceiling seemed to open up and she felt herself floating higher towards an exceptionally brilliant golden light. Suddenly she surged toward it with immense speed. She could hear a voice softly calling her name, "Mia, Mia"... and tears spilled onto her cheeks at the very sound of the voice, for never had she heard her name sound so beautiful, and she knew that it was spoken from the breath of an angel. As she felt herself gliding through the air she was aware of the sweet smell of garden flowers all around her from the heady scent of honeysuckle to the delicate aroma of summer roses. An intensely bright structure of a large individual stood in front of her; but she was not afraid, for somehow she felt that she knew this being from long ago, and yet was unable to remember when.

"You're a messenger from God?" she asked in a voice that she did not recognise as her own. The form moved closer; and she looked into the purest blue eyes that she had ever seen, that shone like blue tinted crystals. She was transfixed as she gazed upon this incredibly beautiful being that could only be an angel.

As though reading her thoughts, it said; "Yes I am an angel, Mia, my name is Azearna and I belong to the order of angelic beings who serve as heavenly counsellors known as Powers. I am here to help you understand that your earthly learning isn't over, and you must return; but first, you must close your eyes and I will show you the truth!" Mia did as she was bid and immediately felt a warm rush of air flow through her just as the angel touched her hand.

Suddenly she felt herself ascending into the air and from somewhere far away she heard the Angel's voice saying, "Remember not the sight, but let your soul never forget." She looked for Azearna; but she had gone!

There was a pale silvery mist all around her and she had the sensation of travelling at an incredible speed. Off in the distance, she could see someone gliding toward her, and as the figure moved closer, she recognised the young man as the driver of the car that had careered into hers, and as they met face to face, he spoke to her.

"Mia" he said, "I lost control of my car and I am sorry for causing you pain. Please tell my wife of our meeting here, it will help her to understand. You will know who she is when you meet her." He smiled, and then he was gone!

Suddenly she experienced an enormous jolt that was immediately followed by surging pains throbbing through her head. Her body felt incredibly heavy, worn and foreign to her in comparison to the magnificent freedom from her earthly bonds that she had experienced just a short time ago.

The next voice she heard grated on her ears in comparison to the sweet sound that flowed from the breath of Azearna. As she became aware of her surroundings she heard someone say, "We've got a pulse, she's back!" Mia was going to live! Of that she had no doubt! Inside, she felt an incredible anger take hold of her as she realised that she was in an ordinary hospital bed. Her body once again ached from the trauma of the car crash. Gone was the beautiful Angel that had spoken so gently to her, and with it went the incredible feeling of love, the likes of which she had never experienced before. As she lay with tubes in her arms and monitors all around her she longed to be by the side of the Angel once more. She tried desperately to remember every detail of her incredible journey for she felt that she had been gone for a long time. She desperately searched her mind to recall the total experience that made her feel that she had definitely left this world and had been granted a glimpse of life after death. She felt a prickle in her arm and then an intense feeling of sheer exhaustion overwhelmed her. In the distance she heard voices but could not make out what they were saying. She tried frantically to keep her eyes, open but finally succumbed to the overpowering desire to sleep and she gave herself up to the darkness that enveloped her like a comforting blanket. For the last few seconds of consciousness she once again saw the face of the Angel and heard her words; "Remember not in your mind, but let your soul never forget."

The next morning as Gerry left the hospital, he was met by a grey October mist that clung to every building and swirled around the street like a slow moving tide He wandered around the car park in search of his car, unable to remember where he had finally parked it, reliving every detail of the last twenty four hours. When he located the car, it looked as though it had been abandoned rather than parked. He jumped in and sat back going over and over the events from the night before. Mia's face swam before his eyes; "Oh thank God she pulled through." he thought. Yet the events of the previous afternoon, prior to the accident, kept rolling through his head like a bulldozer. He had to talk to someone before he went mad!

The buzz of his mobile phone startled him and he quickly clicked the mouthpiece open… "Hello" he responded.

"Gerry, it's Mike. Your mother just called and told us what happened, God you must be going out of your mind, how is she?"

Gerry's relief at hearing his friend's voice threatened to overwhelm him and he struggled for a moment before he found his voice. "Mike, thank God it's you; she's going to make it, but for a while we thought we had lost her."

"Why in the name of God didn't you call us?" asked Mike.

"I was useless; all I could think of was Mia dying in that room, and by the time my parents arrived I was totally out of it," said Gerry, his voice breaking.

"Look, get over here now." Mike said, adding; "Jan will sort you out with some food and you can shower here, throw something of mine on and we'll take you back to the hospital."

"Okay" said Gerry, "but first I'll check in with my mother to see how Alison is doing."

"Fine, we'll see you soon." said Mike, before hanging up the phone.

As soon as Gerry arrived at Mike and Jan's, he showered, and then Jan insisted that he eat some breakfast. Afterwards, he called the hospital to be told that Mia's condition was stable.

"I feel so helpless." said Jan as she put a mug of coffee down on the table in front of Gerry. He looked up at her with tears in his eyes.

"God, how do you think I feel?" he said. "Especially when Mia told me about it before it happened!"

"What are you talking about?" asked Mike.

"I was running late and racing around the kitchen looking for my mobile," said Gerry, "when Mia said that she had just received some email, warning her of an accident. I remember the puzzled look on her face at the time but I wasn't really listening. My head was full of the Curtis case in court later in the morning and I was already pushed for time. I told her not to worry about it, kissed her, and ran out the door. The next time I saw her, she was lying on a stretcher; if only I'd stopped for five minutes and listened to what she had to say she wouldn't be in the hospital fighting for her life."

"For God's sake Gerry, you can't blame yourself because of some email!" said Mike, adding "It's probably some new traffic system sending out details of diversions or something. You've got enough on your plate right now without beating yourself up over an email."

"He's right Gerry." said Jan "Mia and I have been married to you guys for too long to let things like that that bother us. After all, it's usually our fault that you're late in the mornings anyway. And when Mia recovers, the last thing she'll do is blame you for not having the time to listen to her as you ran out the door."

"I suppose you're right." said Gerry. "It all just seems a bit strange."

CHAPTER TWO

⟨decorative divider⟩

Anna Morrison silently reprimanded herself for not carrying through the plans she had made the previous night, as she sat at her computer sending an email to one of her clients, filling him in on the viewing time for a house in Bothwell.

"So much for my long lie and lingering breakfast." she said aloud. Clicking the mouse onto 'send' she rose from her chair and walked across the room and into the kitchen to make some coffee. She glanced out of her window onto the street that was already heavy with traffic and toyed with the idea of throwing something warm on and taking a stroll around the park; it looked so cold and gloomy that she decided to spend her day off in front of the fire with a book instead. As she finished making her coffee, she heard the familiar jingle from the computer altering her to a new email, and slowly made her way back to her desk sipping her coffee as she went, and once seated, she opened her mail. Her first reaction to the message was confusion, followed by anger, and as she re-read it she felt an icy tingle running up her spine; then quickly set about answering the message with the intention of telling whoever sent it exactly what she thought of them. She did not recognise the email address and once she replied she tried several times to send it, but the computer came up with 'address not recognised' and finally, the message vanished from the screen altogether.

"What the hell is going on?"

She frantically searched through a mountain of paperwork on her desk, tumbling most of its contents onto the floor whilst looking for her notepad and pen. Quickly she scribbled the message on a piece of scrap paper whilst it was still fresh in her memory.

It read... "Anna, it is imperative that you contact your brother Andy before mid-day today, tell him that under no circumstances should he leave his home. There will be a violent exchange at the meeting place where the drop off is to take place. He is in grave danger."

Anna immediately telephoned her brother; it rang out ... she tried his mobile and he answered ... "Yep."

"Andy, its Anna."

"Oh hi sis, what's up?" he responded cheerfully.

"What's up? I was hoping you would tell me."

"What the hell are you talking about?" his tone quickly turned irritable.

"Someone in your circle of coke heads sent me an email saying that I was to tell you that something bad would happen if you met at the drop off place today. For God's sake Andy, get out of the whole drug nonsense and get your life in order."

"And end up being a boring little estate agent like you, no thanks!" he said mockingly. "Who the hell sent you this message anyway?" he demanded.

"I don't know, I tried to reply but it disappeared from the screen."

"Look, I'm busy, now, you run along and play little houses with your snobby clients and turn your fucking computer off. " he growled, "And don't phone me unless you want some stuff'! It might help loosen you up a bit!" he added before hanging up the phone. She stared at her phone for a few minutes before tossing it onto the sofa.

"Still as charming as ever!" she shouted aloud. Feeling dejected, she decided that she would have a shower and then go out for breakfast in an effort to banish all thoughts of her brother from her mind. She had tried to reason with him over his drug dealing in the past and had met with the same mind-set. She loved him though, and grieved for the man that he once was, before the drugs.

Andy Morrison drove his Mercedes to the location that he had earlier arranged to meet up with James Thornton. He parked the car and waited. After a few moments, a black jeep pulled into the lay-by. Andy was immediately unnerved since he did not recognise the vehicle, nor the two men who stepped out of it. He rested his hand over the gun in the pocket of his jacket and clicked the car's central locking system on before pressing the window button leaving it only two inches open. In an instant he realised that this was a heist as the taller of the two pushed the barrel of a gun through the space in the car window.

"Unlock the door or it's bye-bye time." the man with the gun ordered.

"Look guys, let's be sensible about this." Andy stammered.

"Just open the fucking door or die." the shorter man with the scars on his face growled. Andy fumbled for his gun and the next instant the window was smashed in with an iron bar that seemed to appear out of thin air. A single shot rang out, and Andy fell sideways, his head and torso slumped over the passenger seat. Andy Morrison was an angry young man who had found drugs early in life, and quickly realised that he could make vast amounts of money as a dealer. And as he lay dying, his anger lived, thriving, and exuding from his every pore with such rancour. Now he could taste the blood in his mouth, and his head felt light and fuzzy as he grudgingly gave up his fight against the inevitable. He briefly thought of his mother, then the darkness claimed him.

He opened his eyes to find himself floating above the car that he had been sitting in only moments before.

"What the fuck's going on? Where the hell am I?" He was aware of several people around the car gazing in through the smashed window.

"It's been a mob killing" shouted one young boy, who went on to beckon his friend from across the street to come and look at the dead guy.

"Hey Frankie, come and see this, he must have been a gangster, but he's nothing but mincemeat now!" the boy yelled excitedly.

Suddenly, Andy felt an incredible pulling sensation hoisting him farther away from the crowd, and just as an ambulance appeared, so his vision altered. First, he saw a faint light far away in the distance. The buzz of the crowd had gone and was replaced by a voice telling him to let himself be led to the light. He tried to spin around, but he was transfixed; as the light moved closer he resisted all the more and screamed in terror as he felt the presence of something unnatural very near to him.

"Get the fuck away from me, what the fuck are you? Where am I?" As his vision cleared, he could make out the silhouette of a hooded grey figure in front of him that seemed to be suspended in air, floating effortlessly. The long robe billowed out around the hem where the feet should be, gently swaying as though it were being blown by a gentle breeze. As his eyes adjusted to the gloomy grey hue, the robed figure lunged toward him at an incredible speed and then stopped inches from his face. It glared at him with eyes that looked as cold as ice, and as dark as the tunnel that Andy now found himself in.

"Is it your wish to avoid the light?" The thing spoke through wasted blackened teeth.

"What fucking light? Is this some piss-head's idea of a joke?" For the first time in the last twenty years, Andy realised true and overwhelming fear. The thing that stood in front of him grinned widely, and the effect was a terrible sight to see. Closing his eyes against the spectacle, he tried to make sense of this ghastly situation and suddenly hope returned as he yelled, "I've had some bad shit! That's it, wait till I get my hands on Beetie Brown, I'll fucking kill him." The figure before him laughed, and from its mouth came a surge like a raging tornado that lifted Andy like a rag doll and hurled him around like a leaf swirling helplessly on the wind. Then, with one wave of its arm Andy found himself suspended in front of the creature; he tried to move but was unable to.   "You have chosen your path;" the thing said derisively, "now it is time to see all that hell has to offer you." It laughed, and a foul smelling black liquid spurted from its gaping mouth that then quickly solidified in front of them, making a black pathway to the world that eagerly awaited its newest lost soul.

Anna Morrison ran through the hospital corridor still in shock, she pushed her way through a set of double doors and found herself at the back end of the accident and emergency department. A pretty, young auxiliary nurse approached her.

"Hi, I'm Jane, can I help you?" she said with the most reassuring smile.

"My name is Anna Morrison, and I'm here to see my brother Andrew, he was brought in about half an hour ago. I am not sure what kind of state he is in. You see, he was shot, and I really must see him as soon as possible

…" Jane put a comforting arm around Anna's shoulder. She could see that the girl was deeply shocked and gently guided her out of the department and into one of the side rooms.

"Have a seat here for just a moment Miss Morrison; I'll go and see what's happening, and I'll also arrange for you to have a cup of tea."

Anna was impatient to see her brother and she started to protest.

"I can't just sit here, I have to see him."

Jane sat down beside Anna and took one of her hands in hers, holding it as she spoke, "Miss Morrison, I know it's hard just sitting here waiting, but unfortunately that's the only thing that you can do right now. If your brother arrived thirty minutes ago, chances are that he may still be in resuss. This is the department that he would initially be taken to. Now the staff will treat and assess him so that all the specialists that he needs will be called to that area. So you can understand how hectic it gets in there." "I'm sorry." Anna whispered as the tears cascaded down her cheeks.

"Oh don't apologise; you're understandably upset, now I'll go and find out what's going on and I'll be back in a jiffy. And I'll send in that tea." As Jane left, Anna managed a watery smile. Five minutes later a domestic arrived carrying a tray with a pot of tea and some plain biscuits on it.

"You're Miss Morrison, yes?"

Anna nodded her head as she said, "Yes I am, and thanks for bringing the tea." The woman placed the tray onto the small table that sat between two chairs and then left. A minute later, there was a knock at the door and a policeman popped his head around it.

"Miss Morrison?" he asked. Anna's face grew pale at the sight of the officer.

"We know this is an awful time for you right now, but we need to speak with you about what happened to your brother today."

"Oh I'm sure you do." she responded mordantly. The officer entered the room closely followed by a female police officer who looked not much older than herself. They pulled chairs closer to where Anna was sitting and sat down.

"I'm Chief Constable Brian Prentice and this is Constable Sharon Dyet; we're very sorry about your brother Miss Morrison. But we need to get some details from you."

Anna stood up. "Are you telling me that Andy is dead?"

"No, no Miss Morrison, all I'm saying is that we need to know when you saw your brother last, and if you knew anything of his whereabouts today. I don't know what his condition is, but I expect the doctor will fill you in on his progress as soon as he can."

The female officer stood up and offered to pour Anna some tea as her colleague continued … "The fact of the matter is … someone tried to murder your brother; and we need to know if he mentioned anything of his plans today, names of anyone that he intended meeting up with perhaps. As I am sure you know, Andy and his contacts are known to us, but like all these cases 'the contacts' suddenly become deaf and dumb during these investigations."

She told the officers about her conversation with Andy that morning and about the email that she'd received. By the time they'd finished their probing, she felt like she'd been on trial herself and she was sure they didn't believe that she hadn't a clue as to who had sent that email. Once they had left, she decided to go in search of someone, anyone who could tell her how Andy was doing. She left the room and started to walk along the corridor. Soon she noticed a man walking in the opposite direction carrying a bunch of flowers. They glanced at each other and to her surprise, she recognised the man as the solicitor she had hired to help Andy through a drugs offence the year before. He also seemed to recall her face, and just as they were about to pass each other he spoke to her.

"Anna Morrison?" he said sounding diffident.

Anna's face creased into a smile; "Mr Brookes."

Gerry extended his arm toward her, and as they shook hands she enquired after his wellbeing.

"How have you been?" she said with genuine deliberation.

Gerry's smile faded. "Well," he said, "up till yesterday my life was great. Now, I'm visiting my wife who was badly injured in a car accident."

"Oh, I'm sorry to hear that, how is she doing?"

"She's out of the woods now, thank God, but last night was the longest night of my life." The dark circles under his eyes confirmed every word that he said.

"But, what are you doing here?" he inquired.

"Andy was shot today." she told him

"Oh my God," said Gerry. "What happened?"

She explained all that she knew, and lastly, mentioned the email she had received.

"Email;" asked Gerry "did you say email?"

"Yes," said Anna, somewhat taken aback at his reaction. "What do you think it means?" she asked.

"I'm not sure," he seemed preoccupied for a moment; "but yesterday," he said in a lowered tone, "my wife received an email, hours before the car accident." They stared at each other in silence for a few moments before they were interrupted by the cheerful voice of the auxiliary nurse who had been looking after Anna earlier.

"There you are, I've been looking everywhere for you." Anna was jolted out of her reverie at the sight of Jane who went on to tell her that a Mr Hillman was waiting to speak to her.

"Oh, I have to dash." she said.

"Of course" said Gerry, adding "I hope it's good news, give me a call later."

Anna said that she would, and hastily followed Jane along the corridor. When at last they reached the Doctors office, Jane tapped on the door and led Anna in; then quietly left closing the door behind her. Mr Hillman rose and shook Anna's hand, introducing himself as the senior neurosurgeon.

"Please have a seat Miss Morrison." he said, inviting her to sit in the chair at the opposite side of his desk. She sat down dreading what he might say next.

"Well Miss Morrison, we have removed the bullet from Andrew's head, but I'm afraid that I have no way of telling what the outcome will be at the moment. You see the bullet entered his right temporal region and lodged itself in the occipital area, and although the surgery was not too complicated in itself, the bullet had already done quite a bit of damage. We can't tell at this moment just how the lack of oxygen to his brain will affect him if he pulls through this. What I am saying is that you have to prepare yourself for the fact that he will probably have suffered a degree of irreversible brain damage, although it is too soon to tell the exact extent straight away. He is critically ill, and in a coma; how long he will remain in his present state is unknown, it could be days, weeks or even months. I am sorry the news is not more positive. I can arrange for you to see him if you wish."

Anna nodded, feeling like she was in some sort of trance, she stood up somewhat unsteadily and was helped from the room by Mr Hillman. The auxiliary nurse was seated outside the door and Anna fell into her arms and sobbed like a child. Later, as she sat by Andy's bed she gazed at his face as if trying to determine what kind of damage had been done, but he looked as though he was simply asleep.

CHAPTER THREE

———◆———

Andy was in limbo caught between good and evil in a terrifying world that he could not escape; his mind battled with the horror that he was enmeshed in. The creature stood in front of him, just grinning with that unsightly gaping mouth.

"You are caught between life and death," it said, "trapped in a world of your own making, expect no mercy here." It moved to one side revealing a doorway that Andy knew he would be entering, and the terror of what lay beyond it petrified him.

"Fear will only attract the 'keepers', who will take you to the pit of the fiend of Gohan" The creature stood aside, and the huge black door creaked open revealing a dim passage sided by huge walls of granite, hanging with lifeless looking ivy trailing desolately down the sides.

"Please don't make me go in there, I'll do anything" he pleaded. The smile on the face of the creature widened and Andy felt physically sick but he had realised a short time ago, that in this place there was no relief from any human sensation, instead they intensified, and the act of vomiting for him was denied. The creature made a rasping noise from its throat and then with a wave of its arm it propelled Andy through the door. The last thing he saw before it slammed shut was the face of the creature sneering at him. Suddenly its face changed, and in its place appeared the face of the twelve year old boy who had died after taking contaminated drugs that Andy had supplied.

Alone in the dim corridor he fell to his knees; he wanted to cry but was unable to. He heard another door opening from somewhere along the corridor and a yellow light spread along the stone slabs beneath his feet like a murky incoming tide. He heard whispering voices in the distance. The voices grew louder as they moved closer, and Andy knew that they were 'The Keepers'.

It was already dark when Anna left the hospital. As she walked to her car she checked her watch and thought she had better call work before they closed; but instead of asking to speak to her manager, she asked for her friend and colleague Clare Higgins, who she knew would not judge her for her brother's sins. She tearfully explained about the email, the shooting, and the meeting with Andy's solicitor at the hospital. When she had finished relating her story there followed a long pause.

"Clare, are you still there?" Anna asked; finally, Clare explained that she too had been sent an email the day before, telling her to spend her time helping herself, not others! She put it down to some sort of joke ... until now!

"Oh my God"! Anna cried, "What's going on?"

"Look Anna," said Clare, "Andy has been mixed up with all sorts of criminals over the past few years, this is obviously scare tactics at work here, he's probably got himself mixed up with the 'big boys' and he has somehow pissed them off big time! Now, they know that the police will be asking all sorts of questions and this email nonsense is probably designed to keep you, and your friends, quiet."

"But what about Mr Brookes' email that predicted his wife's car accident? How could that be tied to a gang?"

"I don't know," said Clare "but I do think you should leave all the supposition to the police; it won't help you or Andy if you start playing the detective. The last thing you need is to start asking questions in the wrong places."

"I know you're right, but it all just seems so weird somehow." she said.

"Look, I'll tell George that you won't be in tomorrow, even he'll understand given the circumstances." said Clare, adding; "As you know I'm on annual leave for the next few days. Tomorrow I'm going over to Sarah and Jack's to help them with their move into the new house, why don't you join us?"

"I'd better not," said Anna, "I think I should be at the hospital."

"I don't like the idea of you being on your own." said Clare. "After all, what can you do at the hospital?"

"I don't know; I suppose I'll feel better somehow."

"Well if you're sure, but call me during the day to let me know what's happening."

"I will," said Anna, "bye."

When she had finished on the phone she started the car up and drove out onto the street. Her thoughts were racing through her head like a runaway train! And she knew that she had to speak to Gerry. Pierce and Brookes Solicitor's office sat above a small row of shops in the heart of Glasgow's West End and a tired Mike Pierce buzzed through to his secretary's office.

"Tracey do I have any more clients this evening?" he asked, hoping against hope that she would say no.

"We have a Miss Morrison waiting to see Gerry but when I explained that he was on leave, Miss Morrison said that she knew all about it and it was vital that she speak to you."

"Miss Morrison;" said Mike, "that name rings a bell. Send her in Tracey, and you get off home; we're running late as it is."

"Thanks Mike; I'll see you tomorrow, oh and the flower basket for Mia is sitting by the sink in the cleaners cupboard so don't forget it."

"Thanks Tracey, see you in the morning, bye."

The moment Anna walked into his office Mike recognised her from her brother's trial the year before. He remembered the details of the case, and how Andy was stitched up good and proper by his so called friends in the drug world. The only reason he didn't go down was due to insufficient evidence. He recalled how devastated she had been that her brother wasn't convicted! Because she'd clung onto the hope that he would get clean in jail.

"Hello Miss Morrison, how are you?" Mike said as he rose from his chair, walked round the desk and shook hands with her. "Please sit down;" he pulled a chair closer to his desk, and Anna sat down. Before he could say any more, she sprang up and started to walk back and forth in front of the desk.

"Mr Pierce" she said, her voice trembling; "I was hoping to talk to Mr Brookes but I expect he's at the hospital." She went on to explain about the emails, her friend Clare, and her meeting with Gerry in the hospital corridor. She stopped pacing and looked at Mike, whose expression was hard to read. "Don't you see we are all linked to these messages, and who in the world could be responsible for sending them?"

Mike was beginning to feel rather uncomfortable. He looked at his computer screen and then back to Anna before saying, "Have you told the police about this?"

"Yes," she replied. "And I don't think they are taking it seriously at all. I really came over in case Mr Brookes had any news, I should have realised that he wouldn't be here." The piercing buzz of the phone made them jump!

"Just a moment." said Mike as he lifted the receiver.

"Mike," Jan's voice was tense; "Come home straight away for God's sake!" He could tell that she was close to tears; and he felt his back stiffen.

"Jan what's happened? Are you okay?"

"It's Shaun ... he got one of those messages just now telling him not to go on the school trip."

"I'm on my way, don't let him out of your sight." He hung up the phone and dashed for the door explaining the call as he went.

"Oh my God!" said Anna. "Can I do anything to help?"

"Here," Mike handed her a card with their phone numbers on it; "call Gerry, his mobile may be switched off if he's in the hospital but keep trying till you get him, tell him to meet me at my house later; and thanks Anna." With that Mike locked up the office and headed for his car, leaving Anna standing alone on the street.

The house that Mike and Jan shared with their son Shaun stood at the end of a tree-lined avenue just off Great Western Road. Jan had been ecstatic when they moved into the rambling property three years earlier, and wasted no time in putting her interior design skills to work. She transformed the five bedroomed house into a shining illustration of her talents, replacing old carpets with maple wood floors, punctuated with fine Persian rugs. The large lounge that had previously stood forlornly hiding behind heavy grey window drapes was now transformed into a bright and welcoming room that had been given a new set of French windows that opened out onto the garden, allowing even more daylight to reach in to touch every corner of the room. Beside the French windows stood an old rocking chair that had once belonged to Jan's father, and was a much treasured possession. The room was contemporary in its style, but cleverly combined with antique treasures that they'd collected over the years. An hour later, Gerry was sitting in Mike and Jan's lounge.

"We have to call the police!" cried Jan.

"The police already know," said Gerry "and where do they start their enquiries? What leads do they have? Some nut is sending emails prophesying impending doom and no one is able to get back to them to find out who the hell they are." said Gerry, as he rose from the sofa. "Where is Mike?" he asked, as though he had just become aware of his absence.

"He's upstairs with Shaun, telling him that he won't be going to Loch Lomond tomorrow with the rest of his class."

Just then, Mike entered the room, and Jan stood up clenching her hands as she asked, "How is he?"

"He's fine, he thinks it's all a big laugh, and he can't understand why he's not being allowed to go on the trip tomorrow."

"And didn't you explain it to him"? cried Jan.

"He's eight years old for Christ sake, snapped Mike. "How can you tell a kid that some spook is sending emails predicting death scenes all over the place? I mean how does it sound to you? It has to be some new fangled sort of prank designed to frighten the daylights out of people and its working."

Mike felt a little ashamed of his outburst and he put his arms around his wife. "I'm sorry darling, I know you're worried, but try not to fret too much." he smiled down at her adding; "He's safe; nothing is going to happen to him."

Shaun Pierce opened the door of his bedroom and listened to hear if anyone was making their way upstairs. When he was satisfied that all was quiet, he closed the door, and ran back to the window of his room and peered out into the darkness. The house next door was the home of his best friend Jack Sutherland, whose parents were both doctors. Although next doors house was at least twenty feet away, Shaun usually had no difficulty in seeing the light in Jack's bedroom through the tall trees in front of the boundary wall. However, tonight he seemed to be having some difficulty in locating the familiar yellow glow from the window. "Come on, Landie." Shaun muttered. Landie was Jack's nickname, given to him by his friends because of his extraordinary ability to 'land on his feet' whenever any of his pranks fell foul of his parents and teachers alike. Jack, like Shaun was an only child, well mannered, and full of mischief. Suddenly Landie's light snapped on! With a sigh of relief, Shaun pressed his friend's number on his mobile phone. Jack immediately answered, sounding harassed.

"Hi, I almost got caught right in the middle of sorting out a bag for you; Mum came into the utility room just as I was putting fresh socks in the hold-all. But I'm not sure that they are a matching pair." he said, adding ... "Still, who's going to look at your feet?"

"Don't worry about those;" said Shaun "just remember to pack me a warm jacket, and don't put that stripy sweater in that your grandmother knitted you." "Okay." said Jack. "Oh I almost forgot" he added … "My mum won't be dropping me off at the pick up point in the morning; it will be Mrs Hardy, the cleaning lady so that's even better."

"Great," said Shaun, "I'm going to set my alarm for six o'clock tomorrow morning so that I can sneak out before mum and dad wake up."

"Good," responded his friend before adding. "Why have they changed their minds about letting you go anyway?"

"I don't really know." said Shaun "Mum ran into the TV room earlier, in the same sort of state that she got into when she lost me in that big shop in London. All she said was that I was not to leave the house under any circumstances, and she was sorry, but the school daytrip was out of the question. Then tonight dad came to my room in a right state, and promised that he and I would go fishing next weekend to make up for it. Grown ups are just plain scary sometimes. Anyway, I have to go no matter what! Because Scratchy Robertson and I are having a punch up, and if I don't go he'll think I'm a coward."

"Oh yes, I forgot all about that, but you can beat him anyway, see you in the morning, bye."

"Bye Landie." said Shaun.

The next day was Friday, and Shaun was up and ready by six thirty. He tiptoed along the hallway and crept down the stairs, then made his way through the house before letting himself out of the conservatory door. The air was icy and a layer of frost covered the ground. Clicking on his torch, he quickly made his way around the side of the house and out onto the avenue. He paused for a moment and looked up at the house before hurrying along to the meeting place.

Gerry and Mia lived at the opposite end of Great Western Road about ten minutes drive from Mike and Jan. Their home was smaller, but just as impressive as their friends. Gerry awoke with the dreadful hollow feeling that had prevailed inside him since Mia's accident two days earlier. He arose and tiptoed into his daughter's room to find her sleeping soundly. As he looked at her face, he realised just how much she resembled her mother, her blond hair lay tangled across her pillow and her perfectly shaped little mouth seemed to be smiling as she slumbered. He stood for a few seconds longer just gazing at her before quietly leaving her room. As he made his way down the scarlet, carpeted stairway with its intricately carved oak banister he could smell the coffee brewing. The kitchen was bright and roomy and his mother was busy setting the table for breakfast. Gerry smiled at her.

"Morning dear," she said. "The coffee won't be a minute, get yourself settled while I cook your eggs."

"You know, the only time I ever eat a cooked breakfast is when you are around." he said.

"Well, I always say there is nothing like a good breakfast inside you to get you started, now come and sit yourself down." He sat down at the table and smiled as he realised that his mother had not changed since his earliest memories of her. He could see himself now in his mind's eye sitting at the big white scrubbed table that stood in the middle of his parent's kitchen. He laughed aloud as he recalled the way his legs used to dangle about six inches above the floor and how Smudge his dog used to try his best to untie the laces of his shoes.

"What's so funny at this time in the morning?" asked his mother.

"Oh I was just thinking about old Smudge."

"Ha, that dog cost me a fortune in shoe laces if my memory serves me right!" said Ruth turning to look over her shoulder at her son sitting at the table, and he looked so vulnerable that her heart ached for him.

"When do Mia's parents arrive?" she asked.

"Their plane gets in at nine." said Gerry.

"Well you'd better get a move on; you know what the traffic will be like. Oh, those poor souls, coming all the way back from America, they're bound to be exhausted, they only arrived there four days ago."

Mike was running late, and as he dashed into the kitchen, Jan handed him a coffee.

"Thanks darling," he said, fixing his tie "where's Shaun?"

"I told him to sleep late this morning, and I think he's taken me up on it. Either that, or he's still sulking over the trip." she said.

"Poor little guy," said Mike while stuffing papers into his briefcase; "I'll look in on him before I go."

"Mike, it's eight thirty" Jan reminded him.

"God I better get off; I'm late, I'm seeing one of Gerry's clients this morning before court." he said as he hurried through the house towards the front door where Jan caught up with him.

"Drive carefully," she reminded him as she kissed his cheek.

"I will," he said, "and you have a good day with Shaun, and try not to worry, I'll call you at lunch time, bye." As she stood at the door waving Mike off, she had no idea that Shaun had left the house two hours earlier.

Chapter Four

At the other side of town Clare Higgins sat in the kitchen of her friend's tenement flat sipping coffee.

"It's amazing just how cold a house becomes when it's stripped of its personality." she said to Sarah, who was looking out the window, hoping to see the furniture van trundling along the street. Sarah closed the window against the cold wind and shivered.

"Subtlety never was your strong point!" she said, and they both laughed.

"I was hoping Jack would be back by now. Do you think he's all right driving that van?"

Clare jumped off her stool and picked up Sarah's coffee from the window ledge where she'd left it, saying, "He'll be fine! Stop worrying! He's probably got caught up in the traffic. I don't think I've ever seen you so agitated!

Now drink this." she said handing her the coffee. Sarah cupped her hands round the coffee mug and smiled.

"I'm sorry. I'm just a bit nervous about the whole thing. I'll be fine when I hear that van draw up."

"You'll be fine whether it comes this instant or not!" said Clare.

Sarah laughed, "What would I do without you?"

Clare thought for a moment before saying, "Oh you wouldn't be able to get out of bed in the mornings; you'd be in a terrible state!"

Sarah hugged her friend as she said, "You can always get me back on track. Here am I, gabbing on about the move and everything connected to it and I haven't even asked how things went with that new guy Steve! So, did the earth move?"

"Not in the slightest! In fact, I was so bored that I almost fell asleep during dinner! I've had more excitement watching paint dry!" said Clare dismally. "I've come to realise that I probably would be better off on my own, so all this dating nonsense has to stop, at least for a while."

"That's crazy! And you know it." said Sarah.

Just then, they heard the sound of squeaking breaks! Sarah dashed to the window and looked out to see John climbing out of the hired van. He looked up at the window and waved.

"Well, that's us all set!" she yelled. Her excitement was almost infectious as she ran to open the door to her smiling husband.

"Come on then," he said, "no time to lose, a new house awaits!"

Clare smiled as she watched then hug each other and thought how great they were together. No other couple in her opinion deserved this new dream house more than these two. She realised that this was one of 'those moments' when she should make herself scarce, and she quietly left them alone while she looked for something to take down to the van. As she studied various boxes stacked along the hallway, she took a mental note to call Anna to find out how Andy was. She was still shocked over the news, and even more so when she thought about that email. She hesitated as her thoughts brought her own message to the forefront of her mind. She had received her email on the same day as Anna regarding Andy but she shrugged it off as scare tactics. She was now convinced that Andy's enemies simply tried to kill him, and sent messages to all those who knew him just to frighten them off telling anything to the police. She noticed a box marked 'kitchen' sitting on top of other larger boxes at the end of the hallway and decided that this was as good a place to start as any. She lifted the box, walked the short distance to the front door and started her descent down the stairs with the box resting on her chest in front of her. Suddenly she lost her footing and tumbled down the stone stairs. The box she had been carrying careered down in front of her, coming to rest on the landing below. She could see the blade sticking up through a split in the box. She screamed, unable to stop herself from plunging into the cold steel of the kitchen utensil.

Sarah and John ran down the stairs to find Clare sprawled over the box. As Sarah unwittingly pulled her friend off the blade, blood spurted out of Clare's chest like a fountain. John called for an ambulance from his mobile, then ran back upstairs to get some towels. Meanwhile, Sarah with tears streaming down her face, tried frantically to stem the blood flow.

Some time later, Clare was aware of noises all around her that were muffled at first, and then gradually became clearer. As she opened her eyes she could see white mist in the distance. Slowly, as her eyes adjusted, she was aware of the figures of many people moving toward her and as they came closer, she experienced the most wonderful feeling of belonging. A figure rose above the gathering, and glided toward her, and as it came closer huge wings appeared out of its back that gently flapped, radiating a golden hue all around it. Her hair was the purest white that Clare had ever seen and her smile was radiant, revealing teeth that shone like precious stones. Gently she took Clare by the hand, and said, "My name is Asha, and I know of your great fear of the death of your earthly body, do not be afraid, come with me …"

Asha held on to Claire's hand and suddenly they were soaring through wispy clouds at an incredible speed. As she looked beneath them, she realised that they were flying through the ages of time When they stopped, they were in a 16th century torture chamber and Clare could see a young woman hanging by her wrists suspended from a rough beam on the ceiling awaiting a terrible death. As she peered closer, she realised that she was looking at herself, Asha waved her hand and the horrible scene vanished, but the stench of blood and fear prevailed.

"Your heavenly name is Andrella," said Asha, "what you have just seen was your very first experience, as an earthly mortal four centuries ago. Your fear of speaking the truth on that day caused your execution and the thing that you most feared came to you. From then on, all your earthly re-incarnations have been overshadowed by your fear of dying. Do not be afraid Andrella; no harm will come to your soul, for it is everlasting. Now, it is time for your return, for you have much to learn."

Suddenly Clare was conscious and in hospital. A doctor standing by her bedside said, "You gave us quite a scare young lady, but you're going to be just fine."

She closed her eyes hoping against hope that when she next opened them Asha would be there, by her side. The noise of the hospital ward told her all she needed to know, she was back, and try as she might she could not escape into that wonderful dream that she had just awoken from. But was it a dream, she thought? She struggled to sit up and was quickly pressed back down again by a nurse who told her to relax. The next minute, the doctor who had spoken to her earlier pushed some fluid from a syringe into a tube that was connected to her hand, and soon Clare closed her eyes, but instead of the beautiful place, she only saw darkness, and she struggled to stay awake, but finally lost out to the medication.

Jan was frantic when she realised that Shaun was nowhere in the house. She ran out into the garden at the back of their home toward the tree house praying that he'd be there, "Shaun, Shaun," she screamed at the top of her voice, "where are you?" She climbed the ladder that was fixed to the side of the oak tree, and pushed the door open to find it empty. Pure panic was beginning to set in as she scrambled back down the ladder ripping her tights on the rough wooden rungs on the way down. When she reached the ground she sprinted back to the house and grabbed the phone and dialled Mike's mobile and to her horror, its familiar jingle sang out from the hall table.

"Oh my God!" she cried, whilst dialling the office; and after what seemed like an eternity Tracey Marshall's familiar voice said "Pierce and Brookes, how can I help you?"

"Oh Tracey, thank God!"

"Jan, are you alright? Whatever is the matter?" cried Tracey, whose heart began to beat wildly, as she silently prayed that Mia hadn't taken a turn for the worse.

"Has Mike left for court yet?" asked Jan.

"Yes he left about a half an hour ago."

"What! He's gone already?"

"The hearing is in Edinburgh not Glasgow, that's why he left so early. Perhaps you can catch him on his mobile."

"He forgot the stupid thing, it's sitting staring at me from the table!"

"Is everything all right Jan?" Tracey's voice was fearful.

"Oh I wish it were, Shaun has gone missing! I think he may have sneaked onto the school bus so that he wouldn't miss out on this silly trip to Loch Lomond. I have to go

Tracey, I have to search for him, but if Mike calls please tell him what's happened."

"Of course I will; but don't you think you should phone the police, Jan?"

"No they don't understand; it's all about these emails. Now I really must go." She hung up … and Tracey was left sitting staring at the phone in her hand.

Jan ran to the kitchen, grabbed her bag and car keys, then scribbled a note for Mike and left the house. Once in the car she took some deep breaths in an effort to control the fast rising panic inside her.

"Stay focused," she said aloud, as she tried to control her breathing. "First stop is the school, and if he's not there then it has to be Loch Lomond." She started the car up and sped out of the drive.

Mia's parents Robert and Margaret Williams waited nervously outside the intensive care unit while Gerry asked if they could all go in to see her, and to his utter delight the nurse informed him that Mia had been moved into a four bedded room the night before, after visiting hour had ended.

"She has come on very well Mr Brookes, and I'm quite sure it won't be long until you get her home." Gerry thanked her and immediately told Robert and Margaret the good news and they all hugged each other excitedly eager to see Mia.

Room 11 was located on the first floor just past the children's ward where a clown was busy entertaining some children who were able to run around. Room 11's door was open and as Gerry popped his head around it he was thrilled to see Mia sitting up looking as fresh as a daisy. She did not notice him at first but when she looked up and caught his gaze she smiled happily at him and he knew that she was on her way back to being her old self again. They all rushed into the room at once anxious to see for themselves that she was really sitting there, and even though she was pale, bruised and a bit weak-looking she was alive. Margaret burst into tears at the sight of her daughter and Robert put his arms around his wife and held her while stroking her hair, something that he hadn't done for years. They had not been getting on recently and their trip to America was designed to put the spark back into their lives. They had often debated about how to tell their daughter that their marriage was all but over, but after the events of the last few days their troubles seemed to pale into insignificance, and in a peculiar way it had brought them closer than they had been for years. They spent the next hour talking and making plans for when Mia came home, and Gerry promised that he would bring Alison in at visiting time that evening. When they had gone Mia, although exhausted, once again retreated into the memory of her near death experience, and she knew that without a shadow of a doubt, that's what she'd had. A nurse came in to check on her

"How are you Mrs Brookes"? Mia told the nurse that despite feeling very tired, she had never felt so good.

"Well that's good" the nurse responded with a smile, "still, don't go doing any acrobatics will you? Rest as much as you can, and don't even think about getting out of that bed on your own. Press the buzzer if you need anything" she said, "but I'll be back in to see you shortly anyway." As she turned to leave Mia's room little Wendy Collins, a five year old from the children's ward was standing in the doorway, "And what are you doing here young lady"? asked the nurse with a note of humour in her voice.

"I wanted to talk to the lady, and tell her all about what Mr McGinty's been getting up to today." She held up a battered looking old teddy bear.

"Just you get back to the other children and leave Mrs Brookes in peace." She turned to Mia and said, "I'm sorry about this, the children's ward is under refurbishment, and these little rascals have been put next door to us."

"Oh please don't send her away, I have a daughter of my own, and I can't tell you how much I miss her. Please let her stay for just a little while."

The nurse relented and told Wendy that she would come back in ten minutes to collect her, then she turned to Mia and said, "Any problems, just buzz and don't fret if she runs out into the corridor, there are gates to prevent them getting anywhere near the doors." As she left the room she stooped down to the child and said, "And no nonsense Miss." Wendy smiled, and the nurse ruffled her tangle of red hair.

The child climbed up onto Mia's bed and said, "Mr McGinty won't eat his dinner, and he hates this place."

Mia laughed softly "Oh I'm sure Mr McGinty will have something nice later to make up for it."

Wendy nodded in agreement. "My kidneys are broken, and I have to come in to get tied up to a big machine that fixes them. But you're the lady that got hurt in the car."

Mia stared at the child, "How did you know that?"

"Shrancanna told me, she said that I was to be nice to you and tell you all about Mr McGinty, but he just sleeps all the time and he only gets a bandage on his leg when I get tied into the big machine. And he doesn't have to lie still and be good."

"Tell me Wendy, who is Shrancanna?"

"She's an angel, silly" the child laughed.

"An angel?" said Mia.

"Yes, she sits on my bed and tells me stories."

"Is she very beautiful, Wendy?"

"Oh yes," said the child, "she has long yellow hair and the nicest smile and she tells me that she will come and take me home soon so that I can see my mummy."

"Your mummy?"

"Yes, my mummy is waiting for me in heaven, don't you know anything?" The child screwed up her face and cocked her head to the side. Mia was stunned!

The nurse walked into the room and ordered Wendy off the bed, "It's time for your nap little lady!" she told her as she took her by the hand and led her to the door.

Before they left Wendy turned around and held up her teddy bear, "Mr McGinty said he loves you, and me too.

Mia smiled at the child and said, "Well I hope to see the two of you later."

The nurse looked at Mia and said, "My goodness! You look radiant, Mrs Brookes; perhaps this little madam has cheered you up after all. When they had gone Mia knew that this child was being looked after by the heavenly forces but she didn't quite understand the reason for their connection … yet.

On the floor above, Andy lay motionless … but inside his head he was very much aware of his surroundings, as his 'Keepers' were waiting to lead him to 'The Place of Unrest'. He was face to face with the demons; he had never seen anything as vile as these creatures, and his fear became incalculable. They swayed in front of him, laughing. Their eyes sat close together in deep sockets and were pure black in colour. Their noses were flat with wide slits at the side that sat above large mouths that were full of pointed teeth. The jaws jutted out far beyond the brows and came to a point that curled slightly upwards, and their heads were bald with no ears protruding from the sides, only slits. Andy trembled before them as they each took turns at prodding him with their thin black fingers.

"Get away from me!" Andy's cry was pitiful. The keepers laughed at the fear in their captor's face as they grabbed him and pushed him toward the door that they had left ajar; prodding him in the back as they walked. The stench of excrement, sweat, and blood hit Andy with such a force, that it took his breath away, and he hesitated at the doors entrance. The Keepers pushed him forward sending him sprawling onto the stone slabs that were covered in filth. He quickly sprang up and wiped his hands on his clothes in an effort to wipe the dirt from them.

"Oh don't trouble yourself trying to clean your hands," said one of the creatures as it moved close to him and peered into his face, "after all, your hands have always been dirty, that's why you're here." It laughed into Andy's face and the sight of its teeth curdled his blood. Slowly it moved away from him and pointed its finger ... saying "this way". The other Keeper pushed him forward. They passed through a short corridor before coming out into a huge circular area, that had been carved out of stone. All around the jagged stone walls were doors of different shapes and sizes. Andy looked down and almost overbalanced jumping back two paces, as he tried to grab onto something solid for the ground beneath him had vanished. The circular area with its cave-like appearance lengthened downwards and expanded above giving a mirror image emergence to this anomalous place. His Keepers prodded him on, harder now, so that their pointed fingers dug into his skin like needles. He was fearful of stepping forward as he tried to come to terms with the fact that his feet had no connection to solid ground. As he moved on cautiously, the doors all around him opened ... and all manner of hideous tormented souls tumbled out; they too seemed to be walking on air.

It was 1pm when Jan arrived at the school lodge in Loch Lomond, and to her despair there was no sign of the coach. The place was locked up and looked as desolate as she felt. She tried to get through to the court building for the sixth time and the lines were still busy. She then called the office.

"Pierce and Brookes" said Tracey.

"It's Jan here again Tracey, I'm at the school lodge in Loch Lomond, the coach hasn't arrived yet and I've been trying to contact Mike, is Gerry there by any chance?"

"He's at the hospital with Mia's parents but I will keep trying both of them," Tracey assured her adding, "any news of Shaun?"

"No, this is so out of character for him to do this kind of thing, what on earth was he thinking?"

"The same as any other boy of his age … they don't think, all they want to do is have fun with their friends; and parents going out of their minds with worry will be the last thing in their heads. He'll be home before you know it looking for something to eat and telling you how sorry he is … you'll see."

Just then the coach appeared around the bend in the road. "Tracey the coach has arrived, I'll call you later." Jan hung up her phone and ran to meet the oncoming vehicle and the moment it came to a halt, its door swung open She ran up the three steps and down the centre isle of the coach searching every face as she went. Mrs Walker, the school's newest teacher followed her.

"Mrs Brooks whatever is the matter?"

Jan was still frantically searching every child but could not locate Shaun. "Where is my son?" Her voice broke … and tears of frustration spilled out onto her cheeks. Mrs Walker, ignoring the distraught woman for the moment asked Carol Simms the assistant teacher to escort the children off the coach, at the same time handing her the keys to the lodge.

"Attention children," she said "Miss Simms will take you into the lodge, please leave the coach in an orderly fashion and no pushing!"

Once they were all off the coach Mrs Walker invited Jan to sit down beside her. She wearily fell into the seat and started to sob uncontrollably ... and when her tears subsided, Mrs Walker asked Jan to tell her what was troubling her so badly. By the time she had related the whole story she felt exhausted.

"Mrs Brookes, Shaun was not at the pick- up point this morning nor were a couple of other children. Your husband did call to let us know that he wouldn't be coming on the trip, and if he had turned up, then he would have been escorted home. I'm sorry you have waited so long for us to arrive but we had a puncture that held us up."

Jan suddenly sat bolt upright. "Mrs Walker who were the other two absent children?"

Mrs Walker thought for a moment, before saying, "William Robertson and Jack Sutherland."

"Jack is my son's best friend."

"Look I think that we should go inside and call the police," Mrs Walker suggested, and Jan followed her into the lodge. A few moments later she was giving a police officer a description of her son and the two other children. As she hung up the phone she thanked Mrs Walker and ran back out to the car and sped away. Ten minutes later a call was put through to Mike at the court telling him of his son's disappearance. He called Jan immediately and arranged for them to meet back at their home.

Sarah Graham sat at the bedside of her friend Clare, and as she listened to her account of her near death experience she became worried that the fall had injured her head.

"I've never experienced anything so magnificent in my entire life," Clare was enthusing, "and the best thing about it is the fact that when we die, there is a beautiful place waiting for us."

"I'm just happy that you're still here, said Sarah "and when you get discharged you're coming to stay with us for a few weeks and then you can put the whole terrible experience behind you, and the near death thing too."

"I'll be just fine when they let me out believe me. But I will never be able to forget my experience with Asha. I feel altered since meeting with her, and I know that I am different because everything seems changed, it all makes sense now."

"What does?" asked Sarah, whilst reaching out and taking her friend's hand in hers.

"This life is just one in many that we have to endure before we learn the true meaning of our existence, our purpose in this 'earth learning' is vital to our souls. Everything has been chosen from the minute we enter this world, and the most remarkable thing is that we ourselves choose our lives from our heavenly realm in order that we learn the true meaning of love."

"Oh my God! You really believe all this heaven thing, don't you?"

Clare smiled at her friend and squeezed her hand. "One day you'll understand." she said.

"Well I hope that day doesn't come too soon! Not if almost dying has anything to do with it." said Sarah. Thoughts of Anna suddenly burst into Clare's mind like an explosion!

"Oh my God I have to call Anna!" she exclaimed!

"Look I'll call her;" volunteered Sarah, "don't you think you should rest? You're not in here with an ingrown toenail you know, you've had a serious chest wound! Now for goodness sake take things easy and stop worrying about everyone else for a change. Don't worry, I'll call Anna and let her know what's happened! I was going to call her anyway." Sarah bent down and kissed Clare's cheek and said, "John and I will be in to see you later. Now rest! And no more thoughts of seeing dead people, angels and all sorts!"

Later when Sarah had gone, Clare was thankful that she hadn't mentioned the scene that she had witnessed only two hours earlier. She had awakened to see white mist swirling around the old lady's bed opposite hers, and as she studied the scene she saw the woman emerging out of her body. Slowly, the woman rotated around so that she was horizontally facing herself, lying on the bed. Between the bodies was a silver cord that stood vertically between them joining them together at waist level. As the woman slowly rose upwards the cord became thinner until it snapped and in that instant two angels appeared, one on each side of the woman. They righted her so that she was vertical and then the ceiling seemed to roll away revealing the most beautiful clear crystal stairway, and on the steps for as far as the eye could see, stood glowing beings that somehow she knew to be family and friends of the old lady's. As they ascended toward the stairway the woman turned and waved at her. Suddenly the light vanished and Clare found herself staring at the ceiling. As she looked across at the now empty bed, she wondered what the woman's life had been like here, and how thrilled she must be to be home.

It was 4pm and already dark; the clouds that had hung forlornly over the rooftops earlier had cleared giving an icy chill to the air. Mike was giving Detective Sergeant James Moor a photograph of Shaun; whilst other officers searched the house for any clue that the boy might have left that could lead to his whereabouts. A computer expert carried Shaun's PC wrapped in polythene down from his room and placed it into a plastic container that was hastily removed to a waiting van. Jan swung her car into their drive just as the computer was being loaded into the back of the vehicle. Her heart pounded furiously in her chest as she leapt from the car onto unsteady legs.

"Oh my God, Shaun," she cried repeatedly as she clung onto the open door of her car for support. Mike, hearing her cries, ran out onto the drive, picked her up, and carried her inside.

"Where is he?" she sobbed as Mike tried to calm her, "where is my boy?" Just then Gerry arrived having been told of the circumstances by Tracey who had finally managed to get through to him. The detective who had been speaking to Mike earlier had received a call on his mobile and walked outside to have the conversation out of earshot of Shaun's parents. When he hung up, he went back into the house and informed Mike that there was every possibility that Shaun was with two other children from his school who had been reported missing. Jan remembered the conversation that she'd had at the school lodge with Mrs Walker about the other two boys not turning up. A glimmer of hope rose inside her as she thought that they might have gone to another friend's house and lost track of time, but her hope was short lived as she reasoned that any mother would call to let them know that Shaun was there, and no such call had come. The doorbell sounded; and a few moments later Jack Sutherland's parents James and Marion joined them. All manner of questions and suggestions were raked over but the terrible fear of what had become of the boys prevailed. It was 7pm when the police left assuring Mike that the minute they heard anything they would contact them immediately. Jan agreed to let James give her a sedative similar to the one that he'd given Marion earlier as she, like Jan, had been bordering on hysteria. Mike insisted that Gerry keep his evening appointment at the hospital, and they agreed to say nothing about the children's disappearance to Mia. Later when Gerry picked Alison up from the house, his mother decided to join Mike and

Jan at their home, even if it were to do nothing but keep the coffee pot going.

Gerry thought Mia looked a little drawn when they entered her room, but as soon as she saw Alison her face flushed with pleasure and her eyes twinkled with excitement.

"We've been missing you mummy," said Alison as she clambered up onto the bed beside her mother.

"And I've missed you too sweetheart, and daddy," Mia said holding her hand out to Gerry and pulling him onto the bed beside them.

"Look mummy I've made you a get well card and we brought you some grapes and chocolate to help you get better," said Alison, excitedly pulling out the squashed grapes, chocolate, and homemade card from her duffle bag. Mia opened her card and smiled at the crooked crayon drawing of an angel!

"Oh she's very pretty, and what's this around her arm?" Mia asked.

"Oh that's her heavenly gift that she was given when she went home." said Alison. Mia and Gerry exchanged concerned glances. Suddenly Alison looked towards the door and her parents followed her gaze to see Wendy from the children's ward standing in the doorway with Mr McGinty clasped to her chest.

"Hello Wendy; come in and meet my little girl and my husband." Wendy walked across the room and leaned up against the bed.

"Hello." said Wendy,

"Hi, my name is Alison Brookes," she slid off the bed and joined Wendy, who was busy staring at Gerry.

"Can you come into my ward and play? We have a talking storybook and lots of toys." Gerry stood up and took Alison by the hand and led her back to her mother. "Perhaps another time, come and talk to mummy and tell her all about your new teacher at playgroup."

"Oh please can't I see the other girls and boys, daddy?" Gerry felt uncomfortable about letting Alison go.

"Oh it won't hurt for five minutes will it?" Mia said quietly.

"Oh I suppose not, but I'll take them in and have a word with the nurses so that they know where we are." said Gerry, as he took both girls by the hand and led them out through the door.

The children's ward looked like a busy playgroup and was very noisy in comparison to the peaceful surroundings they had just left. A nurse came up to them as they entered the ward.

"And who do we have here?" she said directing her words to Alison, Wendy piped up "This is my new friend Alison and this is nurse Emma," she told Alison. "Emma is my very favourite nurse in the whole world and Mr McGinty loves her too."

The nurse laughed and shook her head, "Well, she certainly knows how to get round you, that's for sure." Gerry introduced himself and told Emma that he would be in room 11 should Alison need him. "Oh don't fret Mr Brookes, off you go and have some quiet time with your wife, I'll see to these little ladies." Gerry thanked her and returned to Mia's room to find her staring at the get well card that her daughter had made for her.

She looked up when he came into the room, "Are they all right?"

"Yes, they're under the care of a nurse who seems to know how to handle Wendy." Gerry looked concerned, and Mia recognised the way he nervously nibbled on his bottom lip.

"What's troubling you?" she asked.

"It's that child," he said "I can't quite put my finger on it but she makes me feel quite uncomfortable."

"She's an old soul," said Mia.

"What did you say?" Gerry was taken aback!

"I don't quite know where to begin," she said, "but I have had the most wonderful experience, and now I seem to know things that never would have entered my head before the accident."

"What do you mean?" he asked. She told him of her near death experience and how changed she felt by the whole occurrence. She explained the new understanding she had about their time here on earth, their reasons for being here and the heavenly realm. When she had finished Gerry sat quietly, trying to digest everything that she had told him and his uneasy feeling increased.

"Mia, you're telling me that you actually died; went to heaven, and then came back with some kind of altered perception on life?"

"I realise that it must sound absolutely incredible but it really happened Gerry; and furthermore that little girl from the children's ward is very special."

Gerry looked at his wife as though he was seeing her for the very first time, for this was not the woman he knew. All this talk about death and Angels sent an icy tingle down his spine. He was suddenly so afraid that somehow the accident had robbed her of her senses.

"Oh my God Mia, what has happened to you?"

She smiled in response and hugged his neck. "Darling I know how this all sounds and please believe me when I tell you that this doesn't mean that you and I are sudden strangers. I am still the same person that you know so well and I love you; the only change in me is an awakening; a very profound one that I needed to share with you. You do trust me don't you?"

Looking into his wife's eyes he knew that there could be no doubt of her sincerity and he gathered her in his arms and held her tightly. A little while later they discussed the emails, in particular Anna Morrison's brother, Andy. Careful not to tell her about Shaun's disappearance; he prayed that by the time he went back to Mike's house there would be good news.

Next door, Alison and Wendy had listened to the talking story book that told the tale of two children who got lost in the woods and stumbled into 'The Fairy Glen'.

"I'm so glad that the Fairy Queen saved the children." Alison announced somewhat relieved. Wendy sidled closer to her new friend, cupped her hand to the side of her cheek, and whispered into Alison's ear …

"I know a real Fairy Queen and she has real wings and a face that glows. Do you want to see her?" she said scrambling up from the cushion on the floor.

"Oh yes," enthused Alison.

"Well come on then," Wendy whispered, giving her friend a helping hand up from the floor. "It's a great big secret, so remember not to tell anyone." The girls made their way out of the ward and into the corridor. Wendy looked up and down the passageway before signalling with a wave of her hand that all was clear. Quickly they darted across the corridor and through a door that led into a darkened room. There was a strong scent of lavender in the air and once their eyes adjusted to the dim light they saw a woman lying on a bed next to a curtained window. Neither child spoke as they walked quietly toward the bed, and just as they approached it they were aware of a person sitting on the other side of it with head bowed, appearing to be asleep, wrapped in an eiderdown.

"I can't see a Fairy Queen," whispered Alison who was feeling rather let down. Wendy put her forefinger to her lips and pointed to the person sitting by the woman's bed. As Alison's gaze followed, the figure sitting by the bed looked up at the two girls. Alison's breath caught in her throat as she gazed upon the figure whose eyes were such a bright blue that they appeared to glow in the dim room. When she stood up, what Alison had thought was an eiderdown wrapped around her, gently unfolded to reveal huge wings that were pale blue, and like her eyes, shone brightly.

"Do not be afraid little one," she said to Alison, "my name is Shrancanna. And I am here to look after people who are ill like this lady here." she pointed to the woman in the bed. To Alison's amazement Wendy ran to Shrancanna and threw herself into her arms.

"I looked everywhere for you last night but you must have been back in heaven for your dinner." said Wendy.

"I am not always visible, but I am always here little one so you mustn't trouble yourself by thinking that I am not with you."

"When can I come home with you"? Wendy asked.

"Be patient little one, you will know when the time is right but first, you have a very special task to perform, and you will know what that is soon enough. Now run along and show Alison your new toy."

Wendy left Shrancanna's embrace and walked back across the room to where Alison was waiting. "We better go now," she told her new friend resignedly, and the two little girls left the room and quietly closed the door. Once they had gone, Shrancanna looked at the woman lying on the bed, and gently laid her hand on her chest. The woman sighed, and then gave up her struggle to stay in this world.

Chapter Five

Shaun Brookes and his two friends William Robertson and Jack Sutherland sat in the back of a goods truck heading South.

"You bang on the door this time; my hands are sore." William said rubbing his knuckles.

"Its no good, he's never going to hear us." said Jack dejectedly. "Lets try your mobile again, Shaun." Shaun tossed his mobile across to Jack who tried again to get a signal. "It's no good, we'll just have to sit here till this thing stops."

"I'm starving," said Shaun.

"Well you wouldn't be if you hadn't jumped into this stupid truck so that you wouldn't get caught roaming around Glasgow by your stupid neighbour!" shouted William ... adding, "it's all your fault; just because your mother changed her mind about letting you go on the trip."

"Well it was worth missing the trip so that I could bash your face in, and I'll do it again if you don't shut up!" Shaun yelled.

William was so close to tears that he turned around to face the side wall of the truck in case the others noticed. Suddenly the vehicle came to a halt; the boys sat staring at each other in silence for a few seconds and then started shouting and banging on the sides of the truck in unison.

Tommy Walsh thought the noises were coming from another wagon in the overnight stop; he unlocked the cabin door and slid the metal divider to the open position at the back of the driver's seat so that he could see into the back of the truck, the light was already on, and he couldn't believe his eyes when he saw the boys jumping up and down in the back of his wagon.

"What the bloody hell is this?" Tommy ran round to the back of the truck and unlocked the door. The boys tumbled out as soon as it opened, all yelling at once; we're out, we're out! The bemused driver stood for a few moments, slid his forefinger under his cap, and scratched his head.

"Well, you lot better have a bloody good explanation about this!" he said adding; "where the hell did you lot get on?"

Another trucker who had just parked up, passed by and shouted over to Tommy: "Hey Tom, you started up a crèche on the side?" Tommy took his cap off and threw it down on the ground as the man laughed and headed into the café.

The boys could smell the food: falling to his knees and spreading his arms out in front of him William yelled, "Food, food!" Scrambling up again he then rushed in the direction of the café followed by the other two boys.

"Just a minute you lot: you've got some explaining to do, get back here right now."

The boys stopped in their tracks and without turning round Shaun promised that they would explain everything as soon as they had ordered their food: not waiting for a reaction from Tommy they all rushed forward and clambered through the door of the café.

The boys stood by the display cabinet hungrily gazing at the food when Tommy joined them and said, "Go on then, fill your bellies and then you better tell me how you ended up in my truck. Then, we'll phone the police!"

The boys all looked at each other.

"My dad's going to kill me!" said William.

The woman behind the counter was getting impatient for them to order, "Well, are you going to eat? Or just stand there swapping life stories? I'll die of old age waiting on you lot."

Jack looked at the woman and thought 'what does she mean waiting to get old? She already is!' They all ordered sausage, beans, chips, eggs and extra portions of thickly sliced bread, and large cokes to wash it all down with.

"That will be £12.50." the woman said.

Suddenly realising that they probably didn't have enough money between them to pay for the food, they dug into their pockets searching for whatever they had left, when Tommy told them to go and sit down.

"We've got £5.00." said Jack. Tommy smiled for the first time since discovering the boys and without speaking, he bent his arm pointing his thumb behind him motioning them to sit down. The boys didn't argue and found a table. There was complete silence during the meal, punctuated only by a few burps and gulps.

Afterwards, Tommy said "Right, let's be having you … the whole truth, mind." The boys all looked at one another wondering who would tell the tale.

"I'm waiting," said Tommy.

Shaun spoke up: "Well, it's all a bit daft really. My parents changed their minds about letting me go to Loch Lomond on the school trip today and I was so disappointed that I sneaked out of the house early and waited at the pick up point. Then when Jack and William arrived we argued for a bit: William and I that is, we didn't want to fight in the middle of the street so we went behind some bushes a few streets away to have the punch up. When we got back to the meeting point, the bus had gone! Then we caught a bus into town and went to see a movie, after that, we went to an amusement arcade, and just as we came out of there we saw one of my neighbours, and we ran across the street to hide from him when we noticed your van outside the computer store. A man had just taken a box into the store and we jumped in and shut the doors so that we wouldn't get caught, but the doors locked and we were trapped inside. We thought we would all get into an awful row if we went straight home, but, now we've really done it!"

"You can say that again!" said Tommy. "The fact that you're almost in London is a step for a hint. Your parents must be going out of their minds with worry." Tommy pulled his mobile out of his pocket and called the police. At 11.00pm that night, Mike answered the phone to hear the news that the boys had been found safe and well.

"Just as well he missed the school trip;" said Detective Moor "there was an accident involving a fallen wooden bridge out near the school lodge. Apparently, the bridge gave way, and three kids are in hospital in a serious condition after falling thirty feet. Shaun might have been one of them! We have experts there, examining the bridge for signs of any foul play. I don't want you to relax just now Mike; these emails have to be connected. What I am saying is that some hacker out there may have a grudge against you, perhaps you got him put inside for a spell, whichever way you look at it, he wants revenge, but we'll discuss it in greater detail in the morning. By the way, the guy in the car outside your house is a cop, don't make a move without calling us first. Your little guy should be home around 6am, and the news is he's out cold, tucked up in a sleeping bag in the back of the wagon."

Mike's relief was such that he felt light-headed!

"Thanks John," he managed before his voice broke. When he looked up from the phone now resting on his lap his parents, and Gerry's were all laughing and crying at the same time. Screaming at the top of his voice, Mike rushed upstairs to tell Jan the good news.

At 7:30 the next morning, Shaun walked through the door looking rather sheepish, and before he could say one single word, his mother had gathered him into her arms and held him so tightly that he found it difficult to breathe, and he wondered why mums cried so much. Later ... after telling his parents the story of how they came to be in the truck, he asked if Jack and William could come to tea the next day.

Mia awoke with a start, to find a young man standing in her room. He was very tall with large clear blue eyes; his dark hair reached to his shoulders, and his slim frame was dressed casually.

"Do not be alarmed Mia, I will do you no harm." he said as he sat on the side of her bed. Mia sat up and waited for him to continue.

"My name is Mordrand, and I have been your guardian angel for your past three re-incarnations here on your earth learning. You will not remember me while you are earthbound, but you and I are united in the heavenly realm and will be for all eternity."

"United? but how?" she asked.

Mordrand smiled: "We chose to be born as twins to a family of very poor means two hundred years ago. Our purpose was to give our earthly parents joy in its simplest terms, and that was to show them that the love of their family was greater than the love of wealth and possessions. Fortunately, we succeeded in our mission, and saved our earthly father from murdering his wealthy earth brother who taunted him with his riches but, never shared them.

Souls are precious Mia, and each soul has a learning process to complete on earth before they can move on to higher planes once the earth life has expired. We are here to grow through love; and love has many sides, it is not a simple feeling. It is unconditional!

There is great unrest in the heavenly realm, Mia. The world is changing to such an extent that the souls returning to it are being tempted from their missions by the Sinister Ones. These are angels of the Dark One, whose mission is to collect so many fallen souls that he will rise against the kingdom of Heaven and take over the earth, which will fall into such darkness that the light of day will never again be seen. Your recent glimpse of Heaven has prepared you to help the world to love and so, to live!"

"But, why me? I have no way of saving souls!"

"But you have, Mia. Are you not changed from your visit to the Heavenly realm?"

"Yes, but …"

"Tell me, what has changed in you?"

She remembered the wonderful feeling of the all consuming love that she had felt, during her near death experience; then, the disappointment she encountered once she was aware that she had returned to her earthly body. And later; her feeling of greater understanding of the meaning of life.

Before she could voice her thoughts, Mordrand smiled, and nodded his head.

"I see your thoughts Mia, and, you are more than capable of your task, and rest assured, you will not be alone." Mordrand rested his hand on top of her head, and asked her to close her eyes. As she did so she felt all the pain of her injuries leave her body. "Now sleep, for you have much to do."

When she awoke, it was dawn, and Mordrand had gone! Later that morning, the ward sister called the consultant in charge of Mia's case and asked him to come in and see her. Even though it was Saturday, she felt that he should see for himself the seemingly miraculous recovery of his patient. The consultant stood by Mia's bedside feeling totally mystified as to her phenomenal state of health. He looked up at the junior house officer on his team, and could offer no explanation as to this outstanding state of events.

"Well, Mrs Brookes," he said; "it seems that you have made quite an astounding recovery. To say that I am surprised would be an understatement! But, it seems that you are fighting fit and I don't see any reason to detain you for very much longer. You can go home on Monday if all is well with your tests. I'll arrange for the physiotherapist on call today to pop in and have a look at your movements, but until then don't go jumping around on your own. I will be in the unit around 10am on Monday morning, and if all is well; you can go home then." Mia was delighted! And couldn't wait to tell Gerry the good news!

CHAPTER SIX

———◆———

Upstairs, a nurse had just finished applying moisturizing cream to Andy's lips, and as she turned to leave the room his hand suddenly shot up and grabbed her wrist! She screamed and pulled herself away from the vice-like grip, her heart pounding so hard that she could hear its thumping in her ears. She backed away from the bed, afraid to take her eyes away from her seemingly unconscious patient. With trembling hands she made contact with the door handle and hurriedly backed out of the room. Outside in the corridor she stumbled into Alan Burns, a new porter who had started work in the hospital four weeks earlier.

"You're in a bit of a hurry, nurse Benny!" he cried, trying desperately to hang on to the plastic bag full of red topped universal bottles that he was carrying.

"Oh I'm sorry! I was in a bit of a hurry."

"Oh don't apologise; you can run into me any time you like." he said cheekily, as he winked at her adding; "You look a bit upset, are you all right?"

"I'm fine." she told him, and quickly made her way to the nurse's station, leaving the porter smiling at her. He left the universals in the store cupboard along the hallway. On the way back, he paused at Andy's door, and checked the passageway to make sure that no one was around before slipping into his room. He walked over to the bed, and stood looking down on the pale face lying on the pillow. From deep in his throat there came a rasping laugh and his eyes shone like black crystals. He bent down and put his mouth close to Andy's ear and whispered, "See you will, sleep you won't, will he save you? You know he won't!" Back in the nightmarish place of unrest Andy's hand's shot up to cover his ears as his eyes desperately searched for the owner of the taunting voice! The Keepers laughed; then propelled him into a room off the circular corridor. This room was floored unlike the outside area. He watched as the odd shaped door closed, leaving him alone in the dimness. As his eyes became accustomed to the murkiness, he became aware of tiles covering the floor; the walls were also covered in the same material that looked like clear Perspex. The whole room was dome shaped, and every inch was covered in the tiles.

Suddenly, a light glowed from one of the tiles on the wall in front of him. He sprang back towards the door and sat with his back pressed hard against it. As he watched the tile it seemed to spring into life like a television screen.

As he gazed upon it, a scene appeared of his mother when she was a young woman gently laying a baby in a crib. He could feel a hand lightly stroking his cheek; and as he watched, he realised that he could feel the hands of his mother as she tucked the child into his bed. The next tile to that one glowed on! And he saw his father sitting at the side of a river. His head was bent over something in his hands, and as the picture became clearer he saw that his father was baiting a fishing hook. A young boy ran out from behind some bushes to the right hand side of the scene, and Andy was amazed to realise that it was himself, smiling happily up at his father. All the tiles glowed on in turn, and as they did so, they exposed the whole of Andy's childhood. The whole room filled with scenes of his life, all exactly as it had happened. He watched, unable to give way to the emotions that were trapped inside him. The scenes changed as Andy grew older, and it became more difficult for him to watch. He tried to close his eyes against the visions but to his horror his eyelids would not move, and he understood the role of his tormenting Keepers for he could hear their guttural laugh outside the door. His screams echoed round his hellish prison, and for the first time in his entire life he pleaded with God to help him.

Gerry hung up the phone and gazed at his mother who was standing at the kitchen table rolling out pastry with Alison. She looked up at her son and a worried expression crossed her face as she stopped what she was doing and wiped her hands on her apron.   " G e r r y what is it?" she asked.

"That was Mia on the phone," he told her adding; "and she said that she will be coming home on Monday morning!" His mother's reaction was much the same as his as they stared at each other in sheer amazement!

Alison jumped down from her chair and yelled "Yippee! Mummy's coming home."

"But she's hardly had time to recover from her injuries, I can't understand it." said Ruth. Gerry ran his hands through his hair as he walked around the kitchen, which was his tendency when stressed. For a few seconds he thought about telling his mother all about Mia's near death experience, instead he drew comfort from the fact that somehow her health had seemed to improve dramatically because of it.

"I can't get my head round it!" his mother went on; one minute she looks so weak and the next minute their sending her home!" She added, "Don't fret yourself, dear, we're all here to help when she comes home; I'm sure they wouldn't discharge her if they didn't think she was well enough." Turning back to Alison, Ruth said "Come on then sweetheart, lets get these biscuits cut and into the oven so that we can take them to mummy this afternoon."

Two hours later Mia's parents arrived at the house, and after sampling Alison's biscuits with some coffee they all made their way to the hospital.

Anna had just left Andy's bedside and was making her way down to Clare's ward. Her mind was in complete turmoil, as she struggled to come to terms with the news about Clare. Her legs felt as though they were made of lead as she dragged herself along the corridor. She felt completely exhausted and had developed a dreadful headache. She looked for a lift instead of walking down the stairs and eventually located them at the end of a long passageway. She pressed the button with the arrow pointing in a downward direction and waited. She leaned her head on the wall and gave way to the tears that had been threatening. When they came, they rolled out of her eyes like waterfalls and she could not stop herself from making loud sobbing noises. Suddenly, the lift doors glided open and she would have fallen on her face had it not been for the intervention of a porter who was already inside. Alan Burns caught her as she fell forward stopping her from hitting her head on the rail that jutted out along the three sides of the lift.

"It's all right I've got you!" he said, as he gathered her in his arms keeping her upright.

Anna felt extremely embarrassed as she struggled to concentrate.

"I'm so sorry!" she said weakly. "I felt rather faint for a moment, thank you for your help but I'll be all right in a minute or so."

"It's no trouble at all, but if you don't mind me saying; you don't look at all well." he said, adding; "Would you like me to take you down to Casualty and get one of the nurses to have a look at you?" Before she could answer; the lift doors opened onto a busy corridor. She looked at the porter and managed to smile.

"I'll be okay, really, and thank you for your concern but …"

"You can't go anywhere in your present state." he interrupted her. "At least you can let me get you something hot and sweet to drink. When did you last eat?"

Anna's head was still spinning. "What?" she asked.

"Just as I thought." he said as he took hold of her arm and guided her in the direction of the cafeteria. "What you need is a seat, and something to boost your energy. And then, you'll never have to see me again!" he said pulling a face at her, making her smile. He led her to a seat, told her not to move and then went to the tea bar where he joined the small queue. As she waited she checked her face in her compact mirror and was shocked to see for herself how pale she looked. The tears sprang back into her eyes and she struggled to push them away deep inside her. The porter was soon back and set a mug of hot chocolate and a packet of digestive biscuits down on the table in front of her.

"Look," he said "you don't have to tell me your life story, in fact, you don't have to speak at all if you don't want to; but I would suggest that you drink that," he said pointing to the steaming mug "and eat those."

Anna smiled up at him and noticed for the first time how good looking he was. His thick hair was jet black and his eyes were the colour of sapphires.

"Thank you," she said "as a matter of fact, hot chocolate happens to be a favourite of mine."

"I knew it!" he said, smiling at her, "You look the chocolate type." Anna laughed, and it felt good! They chatted casually while she ate the biscuits and finished her drink. Finally, as they parted company she thanked him and told him that she really did feel better. As she made her way to Clare's ward she couldn't shake off a feeling of disappointment that they didn't arrange to meet again. Clare sat waiting for the nurse to finish dressing her wound.

"I've never seen anything" like it! said the nurse "your wound has all but disappeared; it's astonishing"!

Clare smiled and said "That means I'll be getting out pretty soon then, right?"

"Well if you go on at this rate you'll be up and helping us." the nurse joked.

Anna reached room 14 just as the nurse was leaving and she was surprised to see Clare sitting up and smiling.

"My God, look at you!" she exclaimed, "I can't tell you how happy I am to see you looking so …so well. I was devastated when Sarah called and told me what had happened!" A noise from the corridor outside distracted Anna's attention; looking toward the door she saw Gerry, followed by an entourage of people walking along the corridor.

"What is it?" asked Clare; in answer to her question, Anna suddenly ran out of the door promising to come back in a few moments. She ran along the corridor and caught hold of Gerry's arm.

"Mr Brookes! Please excuse the intrusion, but I really must speak to you; it's very important!" Gerry was taken aback at the sight of Anna's pale face, for she looked ghastly, and her eyes held a look of urgency that concerned him greatly.

"What's happened?" he asked her, fearful of what she might say.

"Another email arrived, and this time it was for my friend Clare Higgins who just happens to be in the ward two doors down." Gerry felt beads of sweat popping on his brow. Suddenly Alison was tugging on his jacket.

"Daddy, mummy is all better, look!" she said eagerly pulling him into the room.

"I'm sorry," said Anna; "I'll see you before you leave."

"No, look … come in and meet my wife." Gerry introduced Anna to Mia, her parents, Jan, Ruth and Alison. After a few moments of polite conversation Anna excused herself and returned to room 14.

"Well, you're a great visitor, I must say!" Clare joked when her friend returned.

"I'm sorry," she said "but something so strange is going on here and we have to get to the bottom of it before anything else happens. Clare, can you walk?" asked Anna.

"Well yes, but where are we going?"

"We're not going anywhere now, but after visiting is over you have to go to room 11 and speak to Mia Brookes. Her husband got an email warning him of her accident, and like you, chose to ignore it! Now she, like you, is sitting up in bed looking as though she has had nothing more serious than a paper cut! What does it mean?"

Clare thought for a few moments and then, for the first time since her near death experience, wondered how many other people had gone through the same or a similar occurrence.

"It is all happening for a reason." she said to Anna, who was watching her intently. "I have been shown life on the other side," Clare told her friend; "and I would not be one bit surprised if Mrs Brookes tells me that she too has been to that wonderful place that we call heaven." Anna sat riveted to her seat as she listened to Clare's account of what happened after she died!

"Nothing happens in this world that is not meant; there is no such thing as coincidence." said Clare.

"But why is it happening to people like you and Mrs Brookes?" Anna asked adding; "And what about Andy? Why is he lying in a coma knowing nothing of what is happening to him; and where is his soul? Is it dead! Or transfixed in time waiting for a miraculous cure?"

Anna had no way of knowing that her brother knew only too well what had become of his soul. Deep within him he was very much aware, especially as he watched helplessly, as his life review relentlessly tortured him with its exact account of his actions on earth. He sat now with his back pressed up against the door with his legs bent in front of him; his arms folded across his knees as he slowly rocked back and forth while moaning softly from deep inside his throat as his past unfolded from the tiles around his hellish prison. The latest scene to emerge was of the day before his wedding; he watched as he was shown the fear on the face of the jeweller, as he held a knife to his chest threatening to plunge it into the terrified man if he did not hand over the diamond and platinum wedding ring from the display case. He felt the man's fear rushing through him like a tidal wave. He screamed out! And the only sound he heard were those of The Keepers outside the door as they taunted him with their guttural laugh. The next scene was that of his wedding night, and every detail was displayed before him as he ravished his new bride's body like an animal that scratched and tore its way to satisfaction; and later … as a reward for her tears of bewilderment … the slap across her pretty face that was to be the first of many.

The vision after that was when he took part in his first drug deal having stolen the money during a post office robbery to pay for them. After that there came the review of his infidelity during his wife's pregnancy, which led him into the night clubs that he later co-owned with another criminal who he eventually murdered for sole ownership of a brothel. The death scene of that particular night took over half of the tiles in the domed room, each showing the multiple stabbing repeatedly. The other half of the tiles showed scenes of his wife giving birth to his daughter on the same night. At one point his wife had called out his name during her agony. Her tortured cry before she died reverberated around the domed room until Andy screamed out pleading for mercy.

After visiting hour was over, Gerry walked along to room 14 and was introduced to Clare. He told her that they were all going to Mike and Jan's for dinner and suggested that Anna come along. If all else failed, at least she would not have to spend the evening alone with her thoughts; she readily accepted, and kissed her friend goodbye. Once alone, Clare slipped her legs out of the bed and stood up, and rather than feeling weak as she had expected, to her surprise, she felt better than she had done in years! She slipped her housecoat on and walked the short distance along the corridor to room 11. Mia was easy to single out from the other three patients for she had a golden aura around her. As she looked up she smiled at Clare, for she knew who she was, as Clare radiated the same light all around her. When she walked over to Mia's bed they embraced instead of shaking hands and both women felt an energy pass between them that neither could explain, but both understood.

"How are you?" Clare asked.

"I never felt better in the whole of my life!" said Mia, smiling broadly. They spent the next half hour exchanging accounts of their near death experiences. They were not surprised to realise that they both felt profoundly changed by the events that surrounded their deaths. Mia explained about Mordrand's visit, and told Clare of how meaningful her experience had been, but that she was still not sure of the reason for it all.

"But Mordrand did tell me that I would not be alone in my task."

"And you won't be." said Clare.

Alan Burns was in the staff room getting changed for his shift when he suddenly felt a surge of white energy flowing through him. He slammed the locker door shut, his eyes turning black with fury. "I will have them!" he growled, sounding almost like an animal. He finished changing and made his way to the porter's room in the accident and emergency department. As he entered the room, the other men fell silent for a moment, and then resumed their conversation ... changing from the subject of him, to talking about the weather. Joe Millar stood up and said that he was going to check reception in case they wanted anything. He was closely followed by Willy McClure. Once outside the room Joe wiped his forehead with a handkerchief.

"That guy gives me the shivers!" he said.

Willy agreed, saying; "He's a weird one and no mistake, and I'll repeat what I was saying before he came in ... he's worth watching."

Back in the porter's room, a call came through from resuss asking someone to collect three units of blood from haematology's blood bank. Burns was on his feet in an instant volunteering to go.

"Off you go, then." said the head porter; happy to see him leave. Once he'd gone ... the two remaining porters breathed a sigh of relief. A laboratory technician waited at the entrance to haematology with three units of blood and as soon as he saw Burns coming through the swing doors he handed them over. Burns about-turned and headed back down to A&E but on the way back, he darted into an alcove under the stairs. He held the blood in one hand, bent his head forward, and blew breath out of his mouth onto the units, transforming them into a deadly poisonous cocktail without altering their outside appearance. He checked the name on the units so that he could locate the patient later.

Back in A&E a nurse asked him to wait, in case they needed more blood but he told her that he had just received another emergency call, and she paged another porter. Burns quickly made his way out of the A&E department and headed for room 11.

Mia and Clare had managed to attain permission from the ward sister allowing them to eat dinner together in Mia's room. They were the only two sitting at the four-seated table as the other patients were unable to get out of bed. They chatted endlessly about life in general … and on the other side.

They had just finished eating the food that Ruth had brought in at visiting time when Mia suddenly laughed.

"Would you just look at this …" she said, holding up one of the misshapen biscuits that Alison had made for her. Suddenly, she looked up towards the door, seconds before little Wendy from the children's ward appeared. The child smiled and made her way to the table. She struggled to get up onto a seat and Clare helped her by lifting her up. She was surprised at how light the child felt, and when she looked into her eyes she suddenly felt a great sadness wash over her.

"Are you all right?" asked Mia.

"Oh yes, I'm fine, but I'm missing my mummy and daddy, they haven't been to see me today."

"Really?" said Clare. "Well I'm sure they will come and see you tonight. And what's this fine looking fellow's name?" she asked; pointing to the child's teddy bear in an effort to change the subject.

"Oh this is Mr McGinty and I think he's lonely because I've been sleeping all day." she said.

"Would you like a biscuit and some milk?" asked Mia. "Alison made them for me and she'll be visiting me again later …" she suddenly stopped speaking as she watched Wendy's cheeky little grin disappear, to be replaced by a worried, almost frightened expression.

"What's the matter?" she asked as she watched the child turn around and stare at the doorway. Both women followed Wendy's gaze and caught a glimpse of Alan Burns as he hovered near the open door for a second before disappearing from view. In answer to her question; the child slipped off her seat and scrambled up onto Mia's lap. Clare shivered, and rubbed her arms, saying how cold it had suddenly become; as indeed it had as the atmosphere became thick with menace. Both women knew that they were being watched by someone, or something evil and Alan Burns was furious! He quickly walked along the corridor cursing under his breath. As he neared the lifts their doors suddenly opened! And he recognised the voice of Will McClure twittering on about his coming fishing trip. He quickly darted into a side room to avoid being seen and left the door open half an inch, so that he could see the corridor from inside without being noticed. Suddenly, Alan's body contorted in pain almost bringing him to his knees. He knew Mordrand was in the room before he turned around to face him. Finally, he spun around, his eyes as black as coal, emanating pure hatred.

"Ah, Zeenkell, we have been waiting for you to show yourself." said Mordrand; "or should I call you Mr Burns?" he added.

"You are not fit to look upon me." hissed the demon.

Mordrand smiled: "Your hatred has destroyed you Zeenkell, but it will never triumph over the kingdom of heaven. Your demons are weakening with every passing hour, for the good shall be protected, and evil will perish!"

Zeenkell laughed! "You utterly stupid, misinformed, piece of filth." he growled. "What makes you think that you and your heavenly master will ever triumph in the world that he himself has created? Look at what he has done! Every corner of his world is now in the grip of violence, perversion, sickness, greed, despair, dishonesty, and crime. He despairs for the world that he himself gave free will to and now, he sends his idiots to save it. But you cannot save something that is already destroyed. Your little world that floats in your master's universe is as fragile as a balloon ready to burst, and when it does, hell will be waiting!"

Suddenly, Mordrand raised his arm above his head and then dropped it down to waist level sending a blue light gushing out from the ends of his fingers. The force of the light hit Zeenkell in the chest and sent his body careering backwards, pinning him onto the wall. As he writhed in pain, his true form momentarily appeared exposing the grotesque features of his face. Suddenly, Zeenkell disappeared, leaving only the stench of a demon lurking in the black mist that prevailed.

Mordrand stood for a few moments while the mist disintegrated completely.

"I will be waiting for you demon." he said, before leaving the room.

A harassed looking nurse from the children's ward entered room 11.

"There you are Miss!" she said, sounding relieved, "I've been looking everywhere for you, and here you are! I should have known you'd be in here. Now come along … you're due to have your medication."

Wendy slipped off Mia's lap and took hold of the nurse's hand; "Can I come and see Alison later?" she asked. Mia glanced up at the nurse who nodded her head indicating that she could.

"Of course you can, I'm sure Alison would be very happy to see you again too." she said. Wendy smiled and waved goodbye as she and the nurse left the room.

"What a strange little girl." said Clare.

"Not strange." Said Mia, "I think she's too wise for her age. She knows she's dying and she speaks of an Angel that will take her home to her mother."

"Do you think she's had a near death experience" Clare asked.

Mia thought for a moment before saying; "Who knows? But I'd guess that she's an old soul, one that has been back on this planet many times over, and now she's waiting patiently to leave it."

"If I hadn't had my near death experience, I'd have called you quite insane for what you've just said." Clare told her.

Mia smiled, and said "You know I have to agree with you. It seems ridiculous to think of a four year old child having experienced so much life, that she is totally at peace with the fact that she is dying. But the thing that really gets to me is the fact that she seems so alone."

"What do you mean?" Clare asked looking puzzled.

"The poor child just wanders around from room to room, even at visiting time. You heard her yourself earlier saying how much she missed her parents, why don't they come to see her?"

"God only knows," said Clare adding; "but I do know that her reaction to that porter was very strange, he seemed to frighten her somehow and that worries me; what do you suppose that was all about?"

"I'm not sure," said Mia "but he made me feel quite uncomfortable too; there was something about his eyes that made my blood run cold."

Both women were surprised by the voice of a nurse walking into the room.

"Hello ladies," she said cheerfully; "you haven't seen madam's teddy bear have you? She's kicking up a storm along there." Clare and Mia both stood up and moved away from the table at the same time.

"I didn't notice her leaving without it." said Mia.

"Just a second." said Clare, bending down between the seats at the opposite side of the table from where

Wendy and Mia had been sitting. "Here he is!" she said, getting back onto her feet. "It must have slipped off her lap."

"That's strange," said Mia, looking totally puzzled, "she must be out of sorts to have let go of him in the first place." she said, turning her attention fully on the nurse; "She worries me; something is bothering that child. I know that she is seriously ill, but she seems very unhappy and insecure today; does she get any visitors?"

The nurse sat down heavily at the table and sighed! "Yes, she does, under normal circumstances! But her mother has had to …"

"Nurse Elgin! Have you found that toy? The poor child is screaming her head off along there." The young nurse sprang up from the seat and looked pleadingly into her ward sister's eyes for this was the second time today that she had been caught sitting down … chatting.

"I'm sorry sister I have it here, I was just letting these ladies know how she was." The sister's face softened slightly and she felt a pang of sympathy for the young nurse, whose love for the child was evident in her every action. She knew that she was finding it difficult facing the fact that Wendy was dying, and was well aware of the attachment she had developed for the child. She was very aware that she would have to tread softly with this young woman who was facing her first experience where there was not going to be a happy ending.

"Well, thank goodness for that! I'll let you have the pleasure of giving the bear back to her; you'll find her in the treatment room."

Thanking her, Nurse Elgin hurried from the room, clutching Mr McGinty close to her chest. Sister Simpson smiled at Mia and Clare and was about to leave the room when Mia said; "Sister, that was my fault just now! I asked the nurse how Wendy was and delayed her, she would have come straight back if I hadn't inquired after the child."

Sister Simpson stopped and turned around saying "I understand your concern for Nurse Elgin, she is a fine nurse and I am not going to reprimand her for having a heart." She smiled, dipping her head slightly, and left the two women feeling relieved.

CHAPTER SEVEN

———

    Anna was seated on the comfortable sofa next to Mia's mother Margaret, and next to her sat Shaun, looking bored as he was still grounded. In front of the sofa stood a large intricately carved, oak coffee table with a glass sheet inlaid on top, that was littered with coffee mugs. Gerry, Mike and Jan were seated on the sofa opposite. Gerry's mother, Ruth brought in a fresh pot of coffee from the kitchen and sat it down on the coffee table before returning to her seat next to her husband William. During lunch the conversation had been mainly congenial and now the mood had shifted to the subject of the emails, but before the conversation seriously got underway, it was suggested that Shaun and Alison go to the television room to watch some DVDs which was met with great enthusiasm.

Once they had gone, the conversation quickly changed to the strange events that had turned their lives inside out over the past five days.

"How are the inquiries into these messages going?" asked Gerry's father. "The police have come up with nothing," said Gerry, adding; "which is hardly surprising given the nature of things. I mean, it's just as though the emails never existed in the first place because no trace whatsoever of them has been found!"

"It's not the emails or the fact that they can't trace them;" said Margaret looking at Anna; "after hearing what this young lady has told us about her friend's experience of actually dying and then returning with details of an existence beyond this world, I have to ask the question that we all want the answer to, and that is … is something supernatural happening here and why? I'm inclined to think that perhaps there is."

Everyone stared at Ruth in silence for a few moments until Anna said, "I agree, and I would have been the last person to believe that there was anything paranormal going on but after listing to Clare's account of what happened to her, I have changed my opinion; you see she is one of the most realistic, down to earth people I know. At first, I was under the impression that the drugs they were giving her were somehow altering her perception of things but, as I listened to the account of her experience, even I had to admit that something mystical had taken place. Clare is not the type of person to embellish anything that she has encountered."

Jan shifted to the edge of her seat, and giving Anna her full attention said, "So what you are saying is that Clare has had a near death experience and come back to tell you about it?"

"That's exactly what I am saying." said Clare.

"But if she has had this experience what about Mia?" Jan turned to look at Gerry who stood up and ran his hands through his hair whist slowly walking around the room.

"Mia did talk to me about flying into some other kind of existence and speaking to some sort of heavenly spectre but I, like Anna, thought it had more to do with medication than fact." He turned and faced Jan, and spread his arms out from his sides in a gesture of bewilderment. "To be perfectly honest, I was just so relieved to know that she was going to live that I … I … thought that she would forget all about it."

Jan thought for a few seconds before saying, "It's not something that one would forget in a hurry Gerry, but I will never forget the way she looked when we saw her at the hospital today."

"What do you mean?" asked Anna,

"She looked positively radiant! Tell me what kind of medication can make you look like that?"

"Well, I for one think it's a load of nonsense!" said Mia's father, "My daughter is alive! Not dead, but alive! You can't tell me that she died and came back to life after visiting people in another world, its ridiculous, absolutely ridiculous!"

"How then do you account for her heart stopping for five minutes while the doctors tried frantically to revive her?" asked Ruth.

"People's hearts stop all the time in these situations and, just as quickly, they start again through electrical stimulus from a machine. The doctors know that the heart will start again after being shocked because they do it all the time. One part breaks down, and they fix it, it doesn't mean that a person is dead for goodness sake!" he shouted.

"Look, let's keep calm about this." said Mike, and turning to Mia's father he added, "No-one is saying that you have to believe this fantastic story. It may well have been a dream, it may not, but, whatever it was we all have the ability to draw our own conclusions. Meanwhile, we have had emails sent to us, even though we have no way of proving it, but if my experience goes for anything, whoever sent them will slip up at some point and then we can put this whole sorry mess behind us."

They all looked at each other in silence. Ruth stood up and walked over to a chair that sat by the window and lifted her handbag and held it to her chest as though she was nursing a small animal. She stood looking thoughtful for a moment before returning to her seat.

Looking at Gerry she said, "I have something to say that might surprise you dear, but I have always felt that the appropriate time never presented itself in the past somehow, but I now realise that the time to tell you has come."

Everyone looked at Ruth, and waited to hear what she had to say … she cleared her throat, looked at her husband who smiled and nodded his head in encouragement. Taking a deep breath, she then said; "I came down with diphtheria when I was seven years old. The doctor kept visiting me at the house and my poor mother was almost insane through worrying about me, and had to keep my three brothers and two sisters away from the sick room which was in the attic. Apparently, I started to see things and talked of a woman in white standing at the bottom of my bed. My fever was so high that I finally lapsed into unconsciousness. According to my mother I was in this state for at least half an hour, and when the doctor arrived, he stood at the side of my bed and slowly shook his head. My mother maintained till the day she died that she knew that I had left this world. She said that I sighed softly, and then she saw an angel dressed in white lift me from the bed and cradle me in her arms before turning and walking through the wall. My mother was hysterical by all accounts, pleading with the angel that only she could see, to bring her child back to her. It was then that I was aware of the scene in the attic as I watched the doctor move away from the bed and take hold of my mother and lead her from the room, closing the door behind them. I remember calling after them, asking them to come back as I was perfectly well and floating at the apex of the arched ceiling. Suddenly, I floated through a tunnel at the end of which was the most incredible light that you could ever imagine. Beside me was the angel who had lifted me from my bed. She was dressed in a white flowing gown, and her wings looked as though they had been fashioned from pale fluffy clouds. Her hair, that was as white as snow, was so long that it reached her waist and trailed down her back between her wings. Her face was ageless and she smiled at me in a way that made me feel safe and warm. When we reached the end of the tunnel she reached out to me and gathered me in her arms, once again carrying me the rest of the way. Then we came out the end of the tunnel and into the most beautiful garden that I had ever seen, and in it were lots of children, mostly of my own age, but some were older looking, and they were playing in what I can only describe as a huge boat made of the most beautiful material that glowed with all the colours of the rainbow, and it seemed to be suspended in air. The angel sat me on the grass and reached into a cluster of beautiful flowers; picked one, and gave it to me. Then another adult figure approached us, dressed in a similar fashion to the angel that had taken me there, except this person was male with short white hair. He smiled at me and then spoke to the angel saying … "Astranna, this child is destined to guide; so she must return in a very short time, but first," he said, turning his attention fully on me … "I have someone here that you should meet."

He held his hand out to me and I took it; then he led me to a corner of the garden where a young girl was playing with a little boy, and as we approached them the girl looked up. I remember feeling that this angel was showing me the life that I would have in this loving place because the girl was my double, my exact image! She ran over to me and smiled, and in that instant I knew that she was in fact my twin sister who had died at birth. My mother had never mentioned that I had a twin and it was amazing to feel my sister's love and familiarity all at the same time. She told me that our earth mother had never gotten over her death and that she had lost her spiritual belief because of it. She then asked me to tell her of our meeting and to reassure her that she was happy. She embraced me and I felt so much love surge through me that I felt that I was unable to breathe.

Suddenly I was back in my bed in the attic and I was gasping for breath. To this day, I have only ever told one other person apart from my husband about my experience … and that person is Mia! I believe that she has had a similar experience; how else could we account for her miraculous recovery? She almost died; in fact, I believe she did die as a result of the car accident; and there appears to have been a change in her that is difficult to explain; but I saw it in her eyes when we visited her at the hospital.

When Ruth had finished speaking, William put a protective arm around her, and it was then that her tears came. Gerry was astonished at his mother's revelation and stood motionless unable to speak.

"Well, now, this is exactly the kind of thing that distorts the true facts." said Robert, directing his words at Ruth. "You see my dear, when you were unconscious it is perfectly feasible to say that you were hallucinating due to the high temperature, and then your brain compensated for the whole sorry business by giving you a pleasant dream; surly you can see that?"

Ruth dabbed at her eyes and looked fully at Robert, before saying; "Well if that was the case, then tell me how we explain this! Ruth slipped her hand into her bag and took out a small silk purse which she gently laid on the coffee table. The atmosphere in the room was tense as all eyes gazed upon the silk purse. Finally, Ruth opened the purse and inside was a small flower.

"Surely that's not the flower …?" said Gerry, as his mother picked the flower up and held it between her forefinger and thumb.

"This was given to me in that garden sixty years ago. When I found myself back in bed gasping for breath, I was still clutching the flower that Astranna had given me."

They all gazed at the tiny flower that was still full of colour shining like a star in Ruth's hand. Their was total silence in the room as everyone gazed at the flower that shone brightly, sending multiple florescent rays of beautiful colours rippling through the crescent shaped petals.

"I have never seen colours like that in my entire life," gasped Jan as she moved closer to examine the flower. Anna stood rooted to the spot with tears running down her face and Gerry sat back down again feeling overwhelmed by his mother's story. Mia's father was speechless as he, like the others, gazed at the incredible blossom that looked like it had only just been plucked from the soil that had nurtured it.

Finally the silence was broken by Robert who said, "I have never been a believer in God, heaven, or anything associated to it but I have to admit that even I find your story incredible and … I apologise for my comments earlier." Feeling extremely uncomfortable and shifting from one foot to another he added; "Of course I'm not saying that I will run down to the church and get down on my knees or anything like that but ..." he threw his arms up in the air and shook his head; "I'm going for a walk, the fresh air will do me good." he said as he left the room looking slightly embarrassed.

"But what of your mother?" asked Anna.

Ruth smiled at the memory; "Oh that was quite Something!" she said. "My mother had put the flower in water and sat it on the little table at the side of my bed. When I had recovered a day or so later, she came into my room and sat on the edge of my bed and asked me where I'd gotten the flower from. When I told her of my incredible journey and of meeting Catherine, she cried and held me tightly in her arms for what seemed to me like hours. After that, she seemed changed ... happier, more confident somehow, and my father changed too, he positively revelled in my mother's new found happiness. Her faith restored, she appeared radiant, and she stayed that way till she died or rather moved into her new life joining my father and Catherine.

Chapter Eight

Mia sat on a seat in her room, idly looking out of the window at the heavy clouds that threatened snow. Suddenly she was startled out of her reverie at the sound of a voice behind her ... "Mrs Brookes?"

Mia spun around to see a woman that she estimated to be in her early thirties standing in the middle of the room. She was dressed in a warm looking three-quarter length grey woollen coat, black trousers, and black polo-necked sweater. She carried a black bag and had a bouquet of flowers wrapped in brightly coloured tissue paper. She was very thin with dark short hair that framed her small well-proportioned attractive face.

She smiled now and said, "Forgive me for making you jump but the nurse said that I would find you here, I hope you don't mind the intrusion, but I just wanted to thank you for spending time with my daughter Wendy. I've just spent the last two hours with her and she was so excited to tell me all about the 'lovely lady in room 11' that I felt that I had to come; you don't mind?"

Mia stood up and offered the woman a chair at the table, "Of course I don't mind," she said smiling. "In fact you don't know how happy I am to meet you." Mia extended her arm out to the young woman and they shook hands.

"I'm Moira Collins, and I'm pleased to meet you, oh these are for you." she said giving Mia the flowers.

"Thank you, that was very sweet of you, but your daughter is the best medicine around here I can assure you." Mia laughed, "She's great therapy. Please sit down …" Moira sat on the seat opposite Mia and a short silence fell between them eventually being broken by Mia, who said, "Wendy must have been very happy to see you today, she was telling me at lunch time how much she missed your visits."

Moira's eyes clouded for a moment before she said, "I know, she was asking all sorts of questions as to why we hadn't been to see her over the past few days. It's very difficult you see, my parents are dead and Brian's parents are somewhere in Australia, they never were close …" Moira stared at her hands that were clasped in front of her on the table for what seemed like an age before she said, "Brian, my husband, was killed in a car accident a few days ago and I have been too busy arranging the funeral and everything … I just could not bear to come to see Wendy sooner, she was bound to ask about Brian's whereabouts. I'm a bit stronger now, and have decided not to tell her, not yet anyway."

Mia's heart was beating wildly in her chest as she gazed at this young woman who was so obviously heartbroken at the loss of her husband, for she knew that he was the man in her near death experience, who told her that she would know his wife when they met.

"Oh my God!" cried Mia as her hand shot up to her throat. "It's you! You're the one he said I'd know when we met, it's you!"

Looking shocked, Moira said, "I don't understand, what you mean?"

Mia tried to compose herself and wondered how she was going to explain to this young woman that she was the driver of the other car the day her husband died. She looked at her now through tears of shock and sorrow and knew that the sooner she got it over with the better. She took a deep breath and told her all about her near death experience and how at the end of it she met Brian.

Moira listened intently to Mia's account and instead of anger as she had feared; Moira's hands shot across the table and clasped onto Mia's and with tears streaming down her face, her only concern was to enquire about how Brian looked and was he in pain. Mia assured her that he looked well but he wanted very much to let his wife know that he was all right. Moira's head bent forward while she gave way to her tears and Mia stood up and walked the short distance around the table and rested her hand on Moira's shoulder. Once her tears had subsided she sat for a few moments drying her eyes, and she looked up at the woman who had just related the most fantastic story.

"I can't begin to tell you how much you have helped me by what you have just told me." she said "You know, from the time that we fell in love at school Brian and I always promised each other that whoever died first would somehow find a way to get a message to the other. You have made me feel so much better Mia, and for that I can't thank you enough. When we married, we decided to try for a family straight away but after four years, we knew that it just wasn't going to happen; finally we plucked up the courage to go for tests and found out that it never would. Then we adopted Wendy when she was just six weeks old and from the moment we brought her home she made our lives so wonderful. We knew about her condition from the start and were determined to give her as good a life as we possibly could and now, the time that we were so dreading has come because she won't last for very much longer, but knowing that Brian will be there for her has eased my dread."

Mia sat back down again and wondered how she would deal with losing Gerry and Alison, and she marvelled at the strength of this young woman coping with it all alone. She searched her mind for something appropriate to say but couldn't find the words and felt relieved when a cheery domestic came clattering into the room pushing a trolley.

"Evening ladies," she said as she set about wiping down the table with a cloth before setting it for their evening meal. "You're not in the worst place tonight, I can tell you, the snow is coming down like there's no tomorrow. They all looked out of the window to see large flakes of snow swirling down on the already white ground.

"Well," said the domestic, "I hope you've ordered something hot for your tea for you'll need it." Her attitude lightened the mood as she left the room whistling.

Moira looked out of the window and smiled, "I'm glad it's snowing," she said, "Wendy loves it, but she'll have the staff tormented when she wakes up because all she'll do is plead to be taken out to build a snowman." She turned to Mia and said "Please don't feel bad for me; I'll get through this; and thank you for listening, I suppose I needed to get it all off my chest."

"I don't know what to say," said Mia, "but I will promise you that whenever you need anything we will be there for you." Moira smiled, and left Mia standing by the window deep in thought.

Alan Burns made his way to the accident and emergency area more determined than ever to carry out his plans to intercept the soul of Mary Conner whose blood units he had poisoned earlier. His whole being was consumed with hatred for Mordrand, his God, and all those who lived in the so-called light of everlasting happiness. Once he entered the unit he quickly made his way to the short stay ward checking the names of the patients on their bed boards as he silently moved along the centre isle, his eyes darting from left to right in search of the dying woman. When he finally located her in a quiet room at the end of the ward he smiled in anticipation as he made his way to her bedside. The woman lay motionless, chalk white, and oblivious to the demon that waited to tear her soul away from the precious eternal light that would lead her to everlasting peace.

"Come on bitch!" Zeenkell hissed, as he grew impatient for the transition of her soul. Then, a soft glow emanated from the woman's body, slowly transforming into her shape as it lengthened and widened. Lifting higher above the body, her soul glowed brightly lingering over its earthly vessel. The demon held his hands out in front of him inches away from Mary's soul and very slowly began to direct its glowing essence nearer to him. Suddenly Zeenkell felt Mordrand's presence behind him and as he turned around to face him his true essence appeared. Mordrand's eyes locked onto Zeenkell's face that had changed from the handsome image that he had taken from a soul two hundred years earlier to his true likeness. He watched as the demon's red eyes shone with pure hatred, the wide nostrils that sat between bulging cheek bones snorted like an enraged bull, saliva escaped from the side of his large mouth that was framed with purple lips that protruded outwards over blackened pointed teeth.

"You come to save this soul, Mordrand?" Zeenkell laughed from deep in his throat, adding, "You know that you will never conquer the dark side, why do you prolong the inevitable? You and your pathetic little angels fly around thinking that your God loves you when all the time he is plotting your doom. He will forsake you Mordrand, and soon you will be begging my father for mercy as your wonderful God casts you out of his so-called kingdom forever."

"Speak not of my Lord," said Mordrand, "for you do not deserve to utter his name, leave this woman's soul and return to your demented existence, and tell Satan that we will overpower him in his fruitless quest to destroy the goodness in this world."

Enraged, Zeenkell turned on Mordrand with one arm outstretched, he pointed to the wall opposite the bed sending him crashing hard against it. Zeenkell raised his arm and the power from it sent Mordrand higher up the wall pinning him there like a helpless fly caught in a spider's web.

"So you think the quest is fruitless? Think again, for we have already countless successes in this world. Just think of the immoral deeds of those you try to save, the lies, the cheating, the stealing and don't forget the murderers among them who take great pleasure in telling tales of their deeds to anyone who will listen. We have already won, Mordrand! Out there is an army, ready and willing to conquer the so-called good people who wish they had the guts to be free to do as they please. There are not enough little Christian saints left to save the world and why? Because your beloved Lord has deserted them."

From the ceiling of the room Mary Conner was aware of two things: she was looking down on a demon standing by her bed, and across from it was an Angel pinned to the wall trying desperately to fight off the invisible force that held him there. The ceiling in the room had opened up like an open flower in the sun, but in its place appeared rolling clouds as dark and angry as the one standing by her lifeless earthly form lying on the bed. Above her there appeared a warm glowing light that beckoned her to it and in this light stood a being that she knew was pure love. She opened her arms and embraced the light and suddenly she became part of its glowing essence; and in that instant, she understood the meaning of life. She rose higher toward the bright being and knew that she stood in the presence of Christ himself, and she threw herself at his feet and wept for every wrong thought and deed that she had ever experienced in her earth form, as her whole life was replayed like a movie in front of her. Her life had been far from perfect and she knew that she had lived it badly, her regret was overwhelming as she wept for the children that she never had. The husband that she had so badly treated by her lying and cheating, whose face seemed to be everywhere in this life review. She saw the pain on his face and then felt the torture that he had experienced in his life by her wrong doing. To her right side there appeared an Angel, and to her left another appeared holding a glass book that held the story of her entire life. The angel held the book above Mary's head and she understood in that instant that her earth life had been a pained existence that taught her that she had been granted her earth form to learn from her many encounters. As she stood between the two angels she realised that she had failed in her earthly journey. Also, as the realisation hit her, she felt forgiveness had been granted by the incredible love she experienced for human kind. The angel with the book of Mary's life held it between her hands and stretched her arms out in front of her, and then dropped the book. The glass shattered into thousands of pieces and as they bounced up from the invisible floor, the shards turned into teardrops that fell down through the ceiling in the hospital room entirely covering Zeenkell; drenching him with tears of regret for a life lived without understanding. The tears burned the demon sending him fleeing from the room cursing God and all mankind. Mordrand fell from the wall where he had been pinned and lifted his face up to the light and received the strength that could only be given from God. The angel to Mary's right asked her if she wished to return to her earth learning; Mary knew that she had to go back and somehow make amends for all her past deeds and bring the love from this beautiful place to her earthly existence and live her life very differently. She felt small, naked and unworthy in the presence of this pure and unconditional love as she once again threw herself at the feet of Christ and wept uncontrollably. She felt his hand touch the back of her head, and the last thing she saw was the face of Jesus before she was plunged into darkness and the only sounds she heard were her own bitter sobs.

Suddenly she felt huge hands pulling on her shoulders; then a rush of cold air penetrated her entire body and her cries turned into that of a new born infant.

"It's a girl!" said a loud voice from somewhere high above her, "and she certainly has a good pair of lungs on her." added the midwife as she wrapped the infant up in a soft white towel and handed her to her mother. The child stopped crying and gazed up into the smiling face of her mother.

"Hello little one," she whispered, as she kissed the child's forehead.

"And what are you going to name this young lady?" asked the midwife.

"Her name will be Mary." the new mother replied with a radiant smile on her face.

A doctor and two nurses rushed into Mary Conner's room wondering what all the noise had been about, but all they saw was a wet floor and the woman lying dead on the bed, staring at the ceiling.

CHAPTER NINE

Shaun stood with his arms folded, leaning against the window seat in the kitchen.

"Hurry up Shaun; you're going to make us late, so stop sulking and get a move on." said Jan as she walked through the kitchen into the conservatory to check that the doors were locked.

"Awe Mum do I have to? Auntie Mia's getting home the day after tomorrow, why can't I see her then instead of going to the hospital with you guys. You know how I hate hospitals!"

"Oh that's a new one!" said Mike as he walked into the room, adding; "All of a sudden, the kid who pleads to be allowed to watch hospital dramas finds that he now hates hospitals." Shaun stood looking forlornly at his parents, who stared at him as though he had just sprouted another head.

"Go to your room and get ready Shaun" said Mike. The boy clicked his tongue and reluctantly left his parents standing in the kitchen. Suddenly, Mike started to laugh; Jan looked incredulous. "What are you laughing about Mike?" she asked.

"Parental control; it seems ridiculous to stop him from going to sit in our neighbour's home when they went through the same turmoil as us. Do you think for one minute they would let them out of their sight, or Jack's room for that matter? Think about it Jan, they're as ruffled as we are over this business, what harm could it do to let him spend some time with his friend?" Just then Shaun walked back into the room and stood silently watching his parents studying each other.

To everyone's surprise Jan said, "Okay Shaun, you can go to Jack's house."

The boy let out a loud WHOOPEE! before he ran toward the door.

"Just a minute young man." said Mike "I'll walk over with you and as soon as we get back I'll pick you up, okay?"

"Thanks dad." said Shaun smiling from ear to ear.

"Come on then, before visiting time comes and goes before any of us get anywhere; we still have to pick up Gerry and Anna." said Mike.

Just as they reached the door Shaun turned and looked at Jan whose smile didn't fool him, and he rushed over and gave her a hug; "Don't worry mum, I'll be fine you'll see."

Jan ruffled the top of his head, "Go on then get a move on, and no horror movies!"

Shaun laughed as he left the kitchen with his father.

Later as they all set off for the hospital Gerry said that he'd had a call from the police to say that all the kids that had been hurt when the bridge collapsed were doing well considering the numerous broken limbs, cuts and bruises they had sustained between them.

"Thank God!" said Jan, and turning to Anna she asked, "How is your brother doing? I mean have they given you any hope of him recovering? "

Anna sighed; "I don't think that he will recover if I'm being totally honest, perhaps it would be better if he did die."

The rest of the journey was spent in comparative silence as Mike concentrated on getting the car through the thick snow. Shaun had settled into Jack's room to watch television, and delve into the tray of goodies that his friend's mum had made for them. They talked briefly of their ordeal two days earlier and then decided to put a different DVD on.

"Okay," said Jack "what do you fancy watching?" I have loads of action movies in the cupboard."

"Great!" said Shaun, "can I have a look?"

"Yeah, in fact, you can choose since you're the guest," said Jack before adding "but don't make a habit of it."

Laughing now, Shaun walked across the room to the cupboard leaving his friend sitting in front of the television. As he opened the door his scream rang out! Jack sprang to his feet sending the bowl of popcorn crashing on to the floor; and in a split second Shaun was dragged into the cupboard by a huge arm with talons sticking out from the end of the fingers; then, the door slammed shut!

Jack, unable to take it in for a few seconds and now alone in the room, screamed at the top of his voice. By the time his parents reached him, he was babbling uncontrollably, all the while pointing to the cupboard door.

At the hospital, Anna sat staring at Andy who looked paler than she had ever seen him since the shooting. She took hold of his hand and felt guilty about her remark earlier in the car. But he was unaware of her sitting by the side of his bed silently weeping; instead, he was only too aware of the horror-filled place that he found himself incarcerated in. He was fast becoming used to the new routine that sickened him to the pit of his stomach. In his dome-shaped room with its inescapable visions he sobbed to be let free of the sights and sounds that were his life, and just as he thought that he would surely go mad the door to his cell would open and he'd stagger out into the stench-filled circular corridor with no visible floor.

Once there, the Keepers asked him how he was enjoying the movie in his cell. All the doors opened simultaneously and each time he came into contact with the other prisoners, as he thought of them, their bodies were slowly changing into hideous creatures with oval-shaped grey faces that seemed to be forming eyes high up in the forehead at both the back and front. He looked down at his hands and to his horror they too were lengthening into grey hued pads with talons sprouting out from the ends of his fingers. The Keepers laughed at his anguish before wielding the whips that they used to hurry their captors along into the next corridor which was filled with the Tormenting demons. Andy had tried on several occasions to communicate with some of the other people who occupied cells such as his, but they seemed to have gone completely insane.

The next corridor was identical to the one that housed the cells except this area was floored and had a huge round table that sat in its centre, and as usual, the table was laden with food. Andy's mouth watered as the aroma of huge platters of roast joints, chickens, pork, duckling, fish and vegetables sat steaming hot ready for the feast. The pain of hunger seemed to be suppressed whilst in their cells, but when released into the arena, starvation hit them with such intensity during these exposures to food, that some of the prisoners pleaded for mercy by promising their souls to the devil and in return, they were taken through a huge arched doorway leaving their cells vacant and ready for its next occupant.

As before Andy, together with the other inmates, was forced to his knees at one side of the arena; behind them were three huge arched doorways. The Keepers sat at the tables and began their feast, grinning at the starving inmates as they ate. One of the demons threw a scrap of meat into the circle of prisoners and there followed a scrabble amongst them for the tasty morsel. Suddenly a fight broke out between the prisoners much to the delight of the Keepers. The two men who were fighting over the scrap of food now half human and half demon raged at each other, wildly tearing at their throats. The larger of the two pinned the other one down and sank his teeth into his throat and began to gorge on the flesh causing frenzied excitement amongst the Keepers. There followed total chaos as the prisoners charged at the table and fought the Keepers for the food and drink. Andy watched as the demons fought the inmates sending food toppling off the table, hurling pieces of meat in all directions.

Suddenly one of the huge doors behind him opened sending a wedge of yellow light into the dim arena and an army of grotesque looking creatures ran in through the door to restore order. Andy quickly slipped unnoticed in through the door and found himself in another circular chamber. He ran across the wide expanse to a door that was left ajar at the opposite side and stood with his ear pressed close to the gap in the door listening for any movement. From what seemed far in the distance he could hear a child's cry. He inched himself closer to the gap and peered round the door and saw a dozen empty cages dotted around the floor space. Quietly, he slipped into the chamber and crouched down so that he was as close to the ground as possible. The wail of the child seemed closer now as he crawled along the floor between the scattered cages, and soon he came upon a trapdoor embedded between the flagstones on the floor. He hesitated in lifting the door for fear of what lay beneath but the sound of heavy boots marching toward the door made his decision for him, and he quickly opened the trapdoor and jumped down through the space. For what seemed like an eternity he slid down through a tunnel that was as black as coal and when he eventually came to the bottom he hit a hard stone platform that was suspended between huge rocks on one side, with more doors imbedded into a granite wall on the other. He stayed crouched where he landed whilst he surveyed his new surroundings. Eventually he dragged himself along the floor commando style to the edge of the platform. He could hear muffled voices rising up through the warm yellow tinted air, and as he gingerly peered over the edge he saw a group of young adolescents lining up smaller children against a wall before giving them orders to dig into the rocks below them with large powered tools. From behind him he heard a muffled sob; turning quickly around he caught sight of a small foot disappearing behind a rock. Slowly, he crawled toward it unsure of what he would find lurking there in the dimness, but just as he reached it he was stopped short at the sound of a child praying to God to let him go home.

Andy froze to the spot; and listened to the child's plea. "Please God let me go home, don't let the monsters get me please, please."

Shaun Pierce sat huddled against the rock and his body trembled in terror as he watched the shadow of a monster crawling closer to his hiding place.

The atmosphere at the hospital was tense as each department became bombarded with incoming calls from staff who could not manage to reach their workplaces because of the thickening snow. A record number of them called to report food poisoning episodes, while accident and emergency were working flat out trying to deal with an unusual amount of attempted suicide patients coming in from all areas.

"What the hell is going on?" shouted one doctor in the busy emergency treatment room who had just sewn up the wrists of a twelve year old boy.

Zeenkell, who now appeared wearing a white coat and donning a fake doctor's identity badge, said "God only knows," as he turned to attend a man suffering from a broken arm. Smiling at the patient he said "and believe me he does know!" as he plunged a syringe filled with an overdose of morphine into the man's arm.

Anna sat at her brother's bedside, staring at him until unable to bear it one moment longer, she hastily stood up and left his room.

Mia felt strangely uneasy, and as she sat listening to the chat of her visitors around the bed her mind kept drifting to the children's ward next door.

"Are you all right?" asked Gerry, worried that she was feeling ill.

"Yes, yes I'm all right, it's just that I haven't seen Wendy's mother this evening and I was wondering if perhaps she was held up with the snow." Suddenly Mia lowered her head and tears spilled out of her eyes and rolled down her cheeks onto the crisp white sheet that was turned down over the duvet cover.

"Come here," said Gerry as he sat beside her and gathered her into his arms. "You've come through so much over the past few days and now it's all getting to you, but you're safe and well thank God, and the day after tomorrow you'll be home."

At that instant Nurse Scott walked into the room; "I'm sorry to disturb you," she began "but I'm looking for Mr Pierce."

"I'm Mr Pierce" said Mike.

The nurse took a breath in, straightened her back, and looked at Mike solemnly before saying, "Mr Pierce, a Dr Sutherland has called to say that you should return home as soon as possible, there seems to have been some sort of an emergency involving your son."

"What do you mean? What's happened?"

Nurse Scott's eyes scanned Mike's face sympathetically before she finally said, "Mr Pierce, it seems that your son has gone from the house."

For a few seconds there was complete silence in the room before Jan sprang up from her seat: "Oh my God not again, please not again!"

"Jan, what is it? My God what's happened?" cried Mia as she sprang out of bed and grabbed Jan by her shoulders. "What is it?" she repeated.

"Oh Mia…" Jan's face had turned ashen and through her sobs she said, "we were going to tell you when you came home and were well enough but Shaun got one of those messages and, and ..."

Mia pulled Jan into her arms and held her tightly saying, "Listen to me Jan, Shaun will be all right do you hear me? It's going to be all right."

Mike laid Jan's coat over her shoulders and led her to the door.

"Go with them, Gerry." said Mia. "Alison can stay here with me, I'm sure the hospital won't mind under the circumstances." Gerry quickly kissed her before hurrying out of the room promising to call the hospital as soon as they knew anything.

"What's happened to Shaun, mummy?" Alison asked.

"Oh he's probably gone out into the garden to build a snowman and got lost in the deep snow." said the nurse who was still in the room.

Anna appeared at the door and looked surprised to find the visitors gone!

"What's wrong?" she asked.

"I'm not sure;" said Mia. "All I know is that Shaun seems to have disappeared from the Sutherland's house, Gerry has gone with them, and he'll call as soon as they know what's going on."

"When can I see Wendy?" asked Alison, and before Mia had a chance to answer her, the nurse said that Wendy was having some treatment at the moment, but as soon as she was finished then, by all means she could see her friend.

"Now little lady," added the nurse, "how about you and I sorting out a cup of tea for your mummy and her friend and then we'll see what's in the cookie jar, how does that sound?"

Alison smiled up at the nurse and said, "I like cookies."

"You do! Well, that's it settled then." said the nurse, giving Mia a reassuring glance before taking the child out into the corridor.

"Oh my God!" said Anna, "what the hell is going on?" She made her way to the window closely followed by Mia. As they stood gazing out into the night, a new fear hit them as they looked at the fast falling snow that had transformed the city into a white wonderland that could easily have made a Christmas Hollywood movie scene look inadequate in comparison.

"They'll be lucky if they make it as far as the car park in this." said Mia. Just then Clare walked into the room.

"Well I don't think I'll see any visitors tonight, how on earth did you manage to get in?" she asked Anna.

"In Mike and Jan's jeep, and though it wasn't too bad getting here, I'm not so sure how they'll fare getting back, there must have been at least another four inches of snowfall since we arrived."

"Something's wrong." said Clare, "What's happened?" Mia related the story of Shaun's disappearance and as she finished speaking, Nurse Scott walked into the room pushing a trolley closely followed by Alison who had traces of chocolate on her top lip.

"For goodness sake, every time I leave this room and come back again, another body appears. Well it's a good job we brought extra cups, is that not right?" she said focusing her attention on Alison who nodded her agreement. "Still," the nurse continued; "at least old Maggie and wee Mrs Taylor got home this morning," she said, pointing to the empty beds "or they would have ordered a full blown buffet bless them."

"Gosh I didn't even notice they were gone!" said Anna as she threw herself down on one of the vacant beds, "at least I'll have a place to sleep for the night if I can't get home."

"Many a true word has been spoken in jest young lady," said the nurse humorously, "and by the look of things you might just be spending the night in that bed providing we don't get any admissions to fill it. Now," she said pausing; "I'm off back to the chaotic ward ... in other words, the children's unit, and before you ask young lady," she said to Alison; "I will come and get you once Wendy has been seen to, all right?"

Alison looked up into the eyes of the nurse and smiled affectionately. "Yes Nurse Emma." she said, preferring to call her by her first name.

When the nurse left the room, there followed a period of silence whilst Mia and Anna poured the teas.

The child's prayer in The Place of Unrest, deep in the dimness of the hellish, stench-filled dungeon somewhere between life and death, stirred emotion deep inside Andy that he had forgotten he possessed. He thought of the child's terror at finding himself in this Godforsaken place and his heart went out to him. He wondered what this boy could have done that was so bad that he should end up in this hellish existence, neither dead nor alive. He stayed still, unwilling to move any closer to the terrified child as the word 'monsters' reverberated around his brain like a boomerang that kept coming back, screaming out the word 'monster'! He looked down at the hands that he no longer recognised as his own and to his horror they looked like hands that would belong to a monster. He was physically changing into one of these creatures that had so terrified him when he was first brought here and he wanted to hide from the petrified child.

One of the doors to his left suddenly opened and eight huge black-clad beasts marched onto the platform. Their heavy-booted feet made sounds like hooves stamping on concrete, and their heads with their two sets of eyes were held erect as they marched into the middle of the platform. Andy stayed crouched without moving as he knew that there was no escape. One of the Sheelka reached its taloned hand down to Andy's collar and picked him up effortlessly and held him at arm's length. When its arm bent, pulling Andy closer to its hideous face, the stench of its breath made him retch. Its black eyes shone with pure evil and the sound of its laugh was as bloodcurdling as the sight of the teeth that were exposed as the mouth opened horizontally across its face.

In a voice that sounded low and threatening it said, "Do you not see that there is no escape from hell?" It held Andy up above its head; "Look at the little frightened mortal who thought that he was a big man on the other side." The Sheelka soldier shook him like a rag doll before dropping him back onto the slabbed platform. It bent its body from the waist and leaned closer to the trembling man as he lay sprawled on the slabs.

"Your terror has not yet begun, mortal, you will be punished for your little detour through the tunnel of mayhem, for this is the way to the Fiend of Gohan, and once there, you will see evil in abundance." The creature laughed and in response the Sheelka Soldiers stamped their feet in unison sending a deafening sound around the arena, the platform vibrating as the heavy boots hit the stone slabs.

Shaun sprang out from his hiding place in terror, desperately searching for a way out of the hellish stench-filled arena and ran straight into the pathway of the Sheelka Soldiers. With great amusement, one of the creatures scooped him up from the ground; holding him at arms length it marched to where Andy was still crouched on the slabs in front of the other solider and dropped him at the creature's feet. Its eyes sought out Shaun's and terrified the boy further by growling like an enraged animal before it sprang upon its prey. Shaun shuffled backwards in terror as the creature lunged at him. Grabbing him by the arm it took him to the side of the platform and held him over the edge. The boy screamed in terror as the creature let go of his arm, sending him spinning down through the murky air toward the floor below. Andy ran to the edge of the platform in time to see the creature extend its arm downwards and some invisible force stopped the boy from crashing onto the floor. Instead, he spun around in mid air hovering above the creatures and children below who stood silently, anticipating the boy's fate. The Sheelka soldier raised Shaun high up into the air with an upward movement of its arm, and pulled him back onto the platform once again. When it set him down on the stone slabs in front of its feet, Shaun mercifully lost consciousness. The creature threw its head back and laughed, then suddenly it stopped and glared at Andy who was horrified to see its eyes turn blood red.

From behind the Sheelka Soldiers looking on, a door opened and an even larger version of the Sheelka made its way through the door and slowly walked onto the platform. Andy's breath caught in his throat at the sight of this latest abomination that stood at least eight feet tall. There was a mixture of animal and a human element in its appearance. The Sheelka stood straight and silent as the beast made its way to the centre of the platform. For what seemed like an eternity, it stared at Andy and the boy, who was still lying on the slabs. Andy stared back unable to take his eyes from the creature's face. Unlike the soldiers, this abomination's face differed. Instead of having two sets of eyes that sat high on the head, one set in front, and one behind, its eyes looked almost human as they were anatomically positioned correctly below the forehead above high cheekbones, but there the human element ended. Its oval shaped eyes were totally black, and glistened like wet onyx. In place of a nose there was a snout resembling that of a bull's which sat above a small black lipped mouth. Its chin jutted out to a point below the snout giving a crescent shape to the face. On top of its head stood one single cone-shaped horn that was as black as coal. The pointed ears that sat at the side of its head moved like a dog's that was listening to sounds beyond human hearing. Its body, like the Sheelka, was broad-shouldered with powerful muscular arms, and a huge chest. Its waist was small in proportion to the body mass and the thighs had an almost exaggerated robot-like appearance that was positioned above huge knees. In place of heavy booted feet, this incubus had three talons that jutted out from hoofed shaped feet at the end of the legs that were covered in coarse hair, and hovering by the side of them was a thick black tail that resembled an eyeless snake. Andy stared up into its hideous face and instinctively knew that he was looking at The Fiend of Gohan.

Beside him, Shaun stirred and opened his eyes, and the sight that he saw sent him scurrying in terror toward the edge of the platform where he stopped, contemplating jumping off down to the depths below. The tears were cascading down his face as he thought of his mother in these last moments of his life before he jumped. He felt the rush of air rippling through his hair and a buzzing sound in his ears, and just before the darkness came, he thought he heard his mother's voice calling his name.

Chapter Ten

⊱─━━━◆━━━─⊰

"This Goddamn snow is unbelievable!" Mike shouted out in sheer frustration whilst trying desperately to steer the jeep through the mountain of snow that was falling profusely from the black sky.

"Hang on a minute, you've hit a drift" said Gerry as he turned toward Jan and grabbed the shovel that she had retrieved from behind the back seat. Slowly he trudged his way to the front wheels that were submerged under the thick snow. As he shovelled through the layers of freezing powder he reluctantly came to the realisation that four wheel drive or not, they were not going to get any further.

Nurse Emma, as promised earlier in the evening, made her way along the short corridor from the children's ward to room eleven to collect Alison. Wendy, although very ill, seemed bright and chatty and as expected had been asking incessantly for her friend to be brought to her ward to play.

On her way, Nurse Emma noticed a porter leaving one of the side rooms that were reserved for terminal patients. Thinking that it was odd for a porter to be in the room, she decided to drop in to see if a nurse was with the patient. She tapped lightly on the door before entering, and to her dismay she realized that the patient was dead! She left the room closing the door behind her and quickly walked back to the ward and phoned a doctor to certify the death. After making enquiries about the patient, and telling senior staff about the porter leaving the room, she once again made her way to collect Alison and take her in to see Wendy.

When she walked into room 11, Mia was pushing the buttons on her mobile phone trying for the third time to contact Gerry.

"You'd be better using the phone at the nurse's station, you'll never get a signal in here." said Emma. She studied Mia closely, noting that she looked pale and troubled.

"Are you feeling all right, Mrs Brookes?" she asked. Mia stood looking thoughtful for a moment before answering the nurse.

"I'm feeling quite all right thanks, its just that I'm really concerned for my friend's son, and you can bet that my husband and the others are stuck waist high somewhere in this!" As she looked at the fast falling snow she felt troubled.

"You get off to the nurses' station and contact your husband," said the nurse "meanwhile, I'll take Alison in next door, and you try not to fret. There must be hundreds of folks stuck out there tonight, and they'll all be helping each other, you'll see."

"Come on, we'll walk down with you" said Clare. Alison tugged excitedly on Nurse Emma's hand and eventually, they all left the room. No one was surprised when the lights went out plunging the corridor into darkness.

"Oh no, that's all we need" said Emma. "If it's not bad enough that the whole place is running on half the staff, just to top it off, the lights go." Alison clutched a little tighter onto the nurse's hand.

"There now" she said soothing the child; "In a minute or two the emergency lights will come on so you've no need to fret." Just as she had finished speaking the emergency lights snapped on, washing the corridor in pale blue light.

"Thank goodness for that." said Clare' adding "Let's get this call made before the lines go." Mia kissed Alison's cheek and reminded her of her manners before heading along to the nurse's station. Anna glanced at Mia as they walked along, she knew that she was concerned about her husband and friends, but something else seemed to be troubling her. This whole situation had them all on edge what with emails, accidents and disappearing children, and now Gerry and the others were obviously trapped somewhere in this freak storm.

As they passed one of the side rooms on their left, Mia suddenly stopped outside the door.

"What's wrong?" asked Anna.

"I'm not sure" said Mia. Her face looked pale and tiny beads of sweat sat out on her top lip.

"That's it!" said Anna cogently "You're going back to bed this minute. The last thing you need right now is to come down with something, you look awful."

"She's right, Mia;" said Clare, "you do look quite unwell. Let's get you back to the room and we'll have someone take a look at you."

"No, I'm quite all right." said Mia fervently "I have to speak to Gerry and once I do then by all means I'll go back and have a lie down if it makes you happy, but please let's just get to the phone." Clare and Anna agreed reluctantly but insisted that Mia walk between them with her arms through theirs for support. The corridor veered off to the left and the nurse's station was situated just around the corner where a nurse was sitting writing something down on a chart. When she looked up she seemed surprised to see the women standing at the console.

"Good evening ladies. What can I do for you?" As she spoke her eyes were on Mia. "Are you feeling all right?" she said as she stood up from her chair and moved closer.

"I'm quite well, thank you." responded Mia hoping that she sounded convincing enough to be allowed to make the phone call. She took a deep breath and said "My husband left the hospital two hours ago with our friends and I need to know if they got through the snow all right."

The nurse folded her arms and looked at the women for a few seconds before saying, "Well if they left here they should have known what they were going to run into. They'd be lucky to have made it out of the car park, honestly, some people just have to learn the hard way." she said sardonically.

Anger welled up from the pit of Mia's stomach and burst through her mouth in inundation as she stared at the nurse's smug face; "My friends were visiting me tonight because they were concerned about my well being. Halfway through the visit they were contacted with the news that their son had gone missing and if you had a heart under that stiff little uniform of yours you would be able to imagine just how bad we all feel for them But as you so obviously seem to be incapable of any compassion then what I have just told you will have fallen on deaf ears but, just so that you understand, I AM GOING TO USE THE PHONE RIGHT NOW! DO I MAKE MYSELF CLEAR?"

From along the corridor a nursing sister heard the commotion and hurried to the station. "Nurse Wilson what on earth is going on here?" she demanded to know.

The nurse responded quickly to her superior by saying, "These women barged down here from goodness knows where and grabbed the phone out of my hand whilst I was in the middle of a conversation with a concerned relative. I told them to wait but this one" she said, pointing to Mia, "was adamant and started to shout that she was going to use the phone no matter what!"

"That's a lie and you know it!" said Anna.

"Quiet, the lot of you." said the sister, adding; "For your information, there is a mobile telephone on all wards for the exclusive use of the patients. I suggest that you return to your ward and ask someone to show you where it is located. We have some very ill patients here and naturally, relatives will contact the staff anxious to know how their loved ones are. Now please return to your ward without any further delay or I shall be forced to call security."

Full of indignation Clare stepped closer to the sister. "Now just a minute Sister," she said, "for your information, this nurse has just told you a pack of lies! When we reached the station she was writing something down on that sheet of paper." she said pointing to the chart. "Under no circumstances did Mrs Brookes take the phone from her, instead, she asked politely for the use of it."

The sister held up her hand stopping Clare from speaking, and just as she did so Mia who had been looking at Nurse Wilson throughout the conversation noticed her eyes glow pure red for an instant as she sat behind the console smiling arrogantly.

Suddenly Mia clasped hold of Clare's arm saying, "It doesn't matter lets get back to the ward NOW!"

Confused, Clare and Anna followed Mia back onto the corridor. "Don't say one word until we get back to the ward." she said, hurrying along in front, with her friends running behind her. Once again as Mia passed the door where she had hesitated on their way down the corridor earlier, she sensed that there was evil in that room. This time, she merely glanced at the door on her right and quickened her step.

Zeenkell stood inside the bedroom door of the doctor on night duty. He smiled with sheer malevolence as he heard the women hurrying along the corridor. He took a deep breath in, and savoured the smell of terror. "Aha the sweet smell of fear;" he said, "always such a delight." He turned to the form of the doctor lying on the bed and laughed softly. "I thank you for your cooperation Dr McGregor." he said as he walked back to the side of the doctor's bed. "My only regret in killing you and taking your identity was the fact that you were in such a deep sleep that I didn't get to see the terror in your dying eyes. Never mind, the night is young and there are so many other souls just dying to get a glimpse of hell. But, I thank you for converting; it is such a privilege to send a soul to the dark side all ready and willing to join The Sheelka." As he turned from the lifeless form lying on the bed he stopped.

"How remiss of me" he said "we can't have two of us roaming around the hospital now can we? Your pathetic little body will have to go." He then stretched his arms out over the doctor's body and lowered his hands, palms downward until they were inches away from the chest. Next he spread his fingers out, trembling slightly, as rays of blue light shot out from his palms hitting the dead man's chest. Slowly the body started to disintegrate, sending flesh falling from the bones that splintered under the force from the light, before dissolving into powder. Finally, all that was left of the doctor was a glowing globe of light that hovered above the powder on the bed that had once been a fit and healthy body. The globe rose higher as the demon looked on. Suddenly it shot up toward the ceiling.

"Ah, not so fast" said Zeenkell as he stretched his arm up and as before, the blue light from his palms shot into the globe. He lowered his arm until the globe caught in his power sat hovering opposite his chest. The demon inside the doctor's body undid his shirt and dug his fingers into the flesh just below the sternum and ripped the chest apart exposing the whole of the rib cage and the upper abdomen. With bloody hands he caught the globe between his palms and as he embraced it, the white shining globe turned black.

"Now that's the way I like my lost little souls;" he drooled, "BLACK!" He then tucked the globe inside the gaping slash before it closed leaving no trace of the violation. Zeenkell rubbed his hands together as though he was washing dirt from them and closed the buttons on his shirt.

"There that wasn't so bad now was it?" he said "Enjoy your trip through the gates of hell and we will meet up again very soon." Just before he left the room he checked his new look in the mirror beside the door. He studied the bearded square shaped face and gazed into the dark brown eyes. "You might have trimmed your beard but still, you didn't know I was coming." His low laugh sounded menacing as he left the now empty room. He made his way to the nurse's station in time to see the sister leaving the console and walking in the opposite direction. Nurse

Wilson smiled conspiringly at Zeenkell as he stopped in front of her.

"All is in order." she said. Back in room 11, Mia sat down on her bed trying to make sense of the confrontation they'd had at the nurse's station. She directed her comments to Clare as she said, "What the hell was that all about?"

Anna and Clare joined her on the bed both confused at the nurse's reaction over the phone scenario.

"She's one of them!" said Mia, "and what's more there is something strange going on in that room we passed; something evil."

Mia studied Clare's face for a moment before saying "You had a near-death experience and just like me, you had yours after receiving an email; Anna's brother is in a coma after she got her message. Why are we linked to these messages? And you're right" she added, again looking at Clare, "something evil is happening in that room and not only there, but throughout this entire building." She shot up from the bed and ran to the window shouting "and look at the weather, its designed to grind everything to a complete halt!"

Anna got up from the bed, shivered and drew her woollen cardigan closer around her body overlapping the sides in front of her. "You guys are scaring me" she whispered. "Shaun is missing! Gerry and the others are out there stranded somewhere probably freezing to death, and my daughter is visiting a child who claims that she can see Angels!"

"That's right," said a voice from the doorway. The three women turned to see Nurse Scott standing just inside the door holding Alison by the hand. There followed a stunned silence for a few moments before Alison broke free from the nurse's hand and ran to her mother.

"It's all right mummy, Nurse Emma will look after us." said the child. Mia picked Alison up and held her tightly as she stared at the nurse. Anna and Clare joined Mia standing by the window and they huddled closer together as the nurse closed the door.

The nurse smiled, and then said, "Do not fear me; I am here to help you. My true name is Acarra and I am a protector of children. I chose to become earthbound three hundred years ago and my vocation is nursing sick children. And, when it is decreed that the soul is to return to The Heavenly Realm which of course is home, I call on Shrancanna, an Angel who assists in the transportation of the children, and places them safely into the hands of the Lord. He welcomes the souls back unto himself, and reviews their lives no matter how short lived. They are then given the choice either to return to earth, or remain in the Garden of Wonder. The souls who return are born again, either to another member of the family that they were originally assigned to, or at a later date, to the parents who lost them. Those who prefer to stay are assigned to help soothe the souls of children who have been propelled into Heaven through an accident or other violent death. These children grow up in the Heavenly Realm and eventually leave the Garden of Wonder to begin their duties as heavenly messengers."

Before Acarra could say anymore, the lights suddenly went out plunging the room into complete darkness. As silence descended, a soft light appeared around Acarra's body and slowly became brighter until she shone like a beacon filling the room with brightness. Suddenly the nurse's uniform vanished to be replaced by a white silky gown. Her already pretty face changed into her true identity and the effect was stunningly beautiful. Her hair that had been neatly pinned up, now tumbled around her shoulders in a white maze, and on top of her head was a single crescent-shaped flower that glowed with radiant colours. From behind her there appeared wings that glowed pale blue and looked as though they were fashioned from paper silk.

Alison wriggled free from her mother's grip and ran across the room straight into Acarra's arms. "I saw your wings yesterday," whispered the child who looked small in the arms of the Angel. Mia slowly sank to her knees unable to take her eyes off the beautiful sight that stood before her. Clare and Anna stood gazing at the Angel in complete astonishment. The only sound to be heard was Mia softly crying.

"Oh dear God," she whispered; "that flower, it's the same as the one Gerry's mother clutched in her hand when she was a child and had been so ill that she passed over. When she awoke she told her mother that an Angel had given it to her in a beautiful garden and she still has it to this day."

Acarra smiled radiantly: "These flowers are found only in The Garden of Wonder," she said. "They are called Moon Fire, named so by a child who passed into the Garden one thousand years ago. She was barely able to speak, as she was only one earth year old. She sat in the Garden surrounded by her new family and plucked a flower, held it to her little cheek and said; 'Moon Fire.' That child's name is Shrancanna."

Suddenly the emergency lighting flickered on! And as it spread its pale blue hue across the room, Acarra's wings vanished and with them the light that had surrounded her, until once again she became Nurse Emma clad in her nursing uniform.

"From now on," said Emma, "you will know an Angel of Light whenever you see one. You will also know the dark ones who are inching closer to us as we speak. We are strong, but the dark ones multiply with every passing hour. Protect the child and stay in your room."

As she turned to open the door Mia asked the question that was in all of their minds; "Emma, what is happening here?"

Emma turned around and looked into Mia's eyes and in that instant Mia felt herself being transported back in her mind to her near death experience. She gasped as if trying to fill her lungs with the last draught of air before plunging into deep water. Once again she heard the beautiful voice of Azearna as she was shown the true account of her time on the threshold of Heaven. And as before, she was now close to the Angel whose voice had the power to fill her with an incredible sense of wellbeing.

The Angel smiled before saying, "Close your eyes Mia, and I will take you back to the place that was erased from your mind when last we stood here."

As before in her near death experience she closed her eyes, and felt the rush of air flow through her once again. A few seconds later she was asked to open her eyes once again, and she found herself suspended high above a group of people hiding in the entrance of a dark alleyway. They were dressed in rags and carried crudely made weapons as they stood poised for conflict. The women and children among them were crying in fear and desperation as they huddled behind the emaciated men who fearfully awaited the approach of their enemies. The sound of heavy boots marching through the ruins that had once been busy streets, boomed louder as they appeared from the corner of the street facing the alley. Mia recoiled in horror as the solders came into view for they were not human! Their only weapons were long talons that jutted out from the ends of fingers that were dressed in black leather gloves that covered huge hands. Their bald oval shaped heads resembled dark brown leather and had two eyes at the front and two more at the back set high on their heads. There was no evidence of any sort of nostrils at the front of their faces and their mouths were elongated slits running vertically from the centre point between the eyes down to the large square chins. Their bodies were tall with huge powerful shoulders and thighs that were clad in black material that resembled wet plastic, which glistened like sweat as they moved. Once they reached the alley, they stopped to survey their prey, and the leading soldier threw his head back and laughed. Its mouth opened horizontally across its face as far as the lobe of its ears that forked out in two points at the side of its head. When the mouth opened like the doors of an elevator, the appearance of the face became even more hellish than before, exposing long razor-sharp teeth that covered the entire lower half of its face.

Mia recoiled in horror as she watched the nightmarish scene unfold below her. Observing her closely, Azearna once again took hold of Mia's hand and immediately the scene changed to one of utter peace and tranquillity. Suddenly she found herself having been guided by the Angel, hovering over the most beautiful garden that she had ever seen. Azearna, with one hand still holding Mia's, and the other gently curled around her waist led her down to rest on warm grass that resembled sheets of emerald velvet. There were flowers dotted across the grass that looked like star shaped diamonds glinting in bright light.

Mia covered her face with her hands and wept! "Why did you show me such horror?" she sobbed.

Azearna regarded her for a few moments before saying: "I took you into the future Mia, a future full of desolation and fear. What you saw were the Sheelka, and they are Satan's army! A ruthless hate-filled hoard of warriors, bred from the evil of the world and instructed by Hell's leader himself to destroy the human race. You have been chosen together with many other mortals to help against the destruction of the world as you know it. If the Sheelka were to conquer the world, the sight that you have just witnessed will become commonplace on earth. If this happens, the kingdom of Heaven will be in great peril and may even fall at the hands of the Sheelka."

Mia gazed at Azearna in sheer astonishment! "But how could this be?" she cried "I have always believed that Heaven was impervious to all that was evil and would remain watertight to any threat."

"Child," said Azearna; "The human race has been given the gift of choice. Many centuries ago, Satan vowed that he would destroy Heaven and earth so that one day, the two would be joined for all eternity. He has worked tirelessly to keep his word, and now, he grows stronger with every passing hour. Never before has it been so easy for the dark forces to guide the lost souls from this earth and turn them into monsters like those you have just seen. He comes in many guises, from the attentive doctor who heals the sick; to the warrior who kills without reason. And his prizes … are the souls that he takes as his own, deep into the abyss of hell adding killing machines to their forces, The Sheelka."

"But you said that man had been given freedom of choice, then surely no peace-loving human being would choose to become part of this evil?" said Mia.

Azearna reached out her hand and softly stroked Mia's cheek, "Listen child," she said; "Satan and his followers come when we least expect them. They may be the friendly old man who sells sweets to children at the corner shop and is in fact filling them full of drugs. Or, the kindly old lady who is helped across the street by some unsuspecting individual, whose body is later found in pieces. The world has changed Mia, changed almost beyond recognition. Hatred for one another builds steadily in every heart and is encouraged by Satan's earthbound disciples. Wars are started by two hearts that are pulled in different directions; good and evil. Brainwashing, violence, perversion and sheer hatred for one another has become a way of life. This is the work of Satan, and his followers are increasing with incredible speed. The time has come when the greatest war of all will occur and that is the war of three worlds ... Heaven, Earth and Hell!"

Mia's heart was heavy with sorrow as she listened to Azearna and she felt an overpowering hopelessness well up inside her as the tears tumbled down her cheeks.

"But how can mere mortals such as myself find the strength and power to overcome those monsters?"

"Your soul is the answer." said Azearna. Suddenly Mia was aware of people walking around the beautiful garden seemingly oblivious to herself and Azearna sitting on the grass.

"See how happy they are;" said the Angel, "see how their children play without fear, and see how they lay their baskets of food on the grass without fear of those who would poison them?"

Mia felt confused and asked, "Where did they come from? And why can they not see us?" Azearna stood up and helped Mia to her feet.

"They do not see us because they have not yet been born. I have taken you into the future. The first vision was the future governed by Satan and the Sheelka. This vision," she said, spreading her arm out in front of her, "is the future without evil's intervention if the Sheelka lose their battle. Too many souls have lost their fight against evil and have then become part of it. The time has come to fight the forces that are emptying the earth and leaving behind the stench of death.

Mia watched as Azearna laid her hand against her chest and closed her eyes. When she took her hand away, there in the palm of her hand sat a tiny glowing orb. The Angel then moved closer to Mia and pressed the globe with the flat of her hand onto Mia's chest. As she stood looking into the Angel's pure blue eyes she felt the most wonderful sensation of love for mankind flow through every nerve in her body. She gasped as the feeling grew stronger and profoundly sensational with every passing second. She closed her eyes savouring the wonderful sensations of pure bliss but when she opened them again, Azearna was gone!

Mia quickly realised that she was once again in the hospital room with her daughter Anna, Clare and Nurse Emma.

"She's gasping for air!" Anna cried frantically to the nurse.

"And she can't stand!" cried Clare as she slid a chair under Mia's buckling legs.

The nurse simply smiled before saying, "She has never felt better in her entire life, of that I can assure you." Just then a scream rang out from somewhere along the corridor sending the nurse rushing from the room quickly followed by Clare. Anna stayed in the room with Mia as did Alison who had been frightened by the noise. The two women raced into the corridor in time to see a terrified looking nurse dashing out of one of the side rooms, her feet sliding on blood as she fled.

"Oh my God!" cried Clare as she instinctively pressed her back up against the wall and inched her way along behind Nurse Emma. The sight that met them when they reached the open door was one of sheer horror as the room's occupant lay headless on the blood soaked bed. His bowel had been completely removed and wrapped around the overhead light above the bed where it dripped blood into the gaping hole in the lower abdomen. The head sat on the side cabinet next to the carnage with his still-steaming heart wedged into the gaping mouth, his eyes wide with terror.

Clare vomited where she stood and the nurse grabbed her by her shoulder as she ran back along the corridor trailing Clare behind her. Once outside the children's ward Emma reached into her pocket and offered Clare a facial wipe.

"Listen to me," said the nurse; "I want you to stay in the children's ward." Clare was still reeling from the sight in the side room and the nurse took hold of her by her shoulders and shook her. "CLARE!" she shouted, "You must be strong and listen to what I have to say to you. Now, you must stay by the side of Wendy's bed and protect her. Do you understand?"

Clare nodded her head and the nurse repeated her words; "Wendy must be protected." Clare looked into the ward through the glass window on the top half of the door and immediately located Wendy's bed at the very end of the ward next to the huge bay window. She gasped as she looked at the child sitting there quietly reading a book, for her body was surrounded by a silver light glowing brightly.

"Emma," she said, turning to the nurse … but Emma had gone!

Gerry, Mike and Jan had abandoned the jeep next to countless other vehicles in the middle of the City centre. The whole area had ground to a complete standstill and people were trudging though the snow going off in all directions in search of somewhere to spend the night. Shop keepers opened their doors to let people in from the freezing streets, and pubs along the way were overflowing with stranded travellers searching for heat. They tried to squeeze into countless pubs and hotels along the snow packed streets without success as each one they stopped at was already overflowing with cold and hungry people seeking shelter. Eventually they inadvertently stumbled onto the doorstep of a small guest house where they paused on the steps for a rest. On the same side of the street a young woman struggled to make her way through the drifting snow toward the entrance of the guest house. Both Mike and Gerry ventured off their concrete ledge where the snow was only about twelve inches deep and once again plunged into the snow to help the woman up onto the steps.

"Thank you" she said breathlessly as they helped her. "I thought I'd make my way down to see if my parents were okay," she added "and I swear to God, there has been at least another two feet of snowfall since I set off. Still never mind, at least I made it." She struggled up onto the third step and turning to Gerry said, "If you're stranded, I'm sure my parents could squeeze you in." She pointed to a door with a warm welcoming yellow glow steaming out from behind the leaded glass circular panel in its centre. No one hung around for a second invitation as they all clambered towards the door.

As soon as they were warm, dry and settled in the only vacant room that was left Gerry called the Sutherlands' mobile. He clicked the mouthpiece of his mobile phone shut and turned to Mike and Jan who stood close by him waiting anxiously for news of Shaun.

"The Sutherlands have no explanation of how Shaun vanished. They just can't get any sense out of Jack, who insists that Shaun disappeared through a cupboard! The phone lines are down but they have managed to contact the police and some officers are struggling their way through the snow on skis to get to the house. They've given Jack two milligrams of diazepam to calm him down. They reckon that once he's slept it off, they may be able to get some sense out of him.

Mike paced the small room holding his head in his hands while Gerry poured some drinks. "I should never have insisted that he go over there in the first place. For God's sake what was I thinking? What kind of people are they to let a kid just vanish from their house without a trace? And this cupboard nonsense! What the hell is their kid on?"

"Here drink this." said Gerry handing Mike a generous glass of brandy, "You can't shoot off at the Sutherlands, Mike!" he said. "Christ, we've known them for years and they are both well respected doctors, not to mention good and responsible parents. They're well aware of what we've all been through over the past week. Their kid went missing too, and I'm quite sure that because of that they took every precaution to make sure that the boys were safe. I reckon Shaun's gone over to your place to get some CDs or something. His mobile is at the Sutherlands' house so if he decided to stay in your house instead of trudging back through the snow then he would try to contact Jack. There must be at least six feet of the stuff on the ground by now and it's still coming down. If you ask me, he's done the sensible thing and stayed indoors."

"Of course!" said Jan, who had been sitting on the edge of the bed staring at the wall but listening intently whilst finishing off her second glass of brandy. "Of course." she repeated as she sprang up from the bed and headed for the bottle of brandy sitting on the small round table that stood in front of the window. Gerry and Mike exchanged concerned glances as Jan filled her glass and sat back down again.

"It's just as Gerry said, Mike." she said, without looking at any of them. "Shaun is safe at home, he's safe, he's safe." she said, all the while drinking down large amounts of the bronze liquid. As she sat on the bed with her back toward Mike and Gerry she gently swayed back and forth as she repeated her words; "He's safe ..." Mike made to move toward her but Gerry stopped him by holding his arm up and touching the sleeve of his jacket.

"Leave her Mike;" he whispered, adding, "she's better off sitting there imagining Shaun tucked up in front of the fire …" He stopped and looked into Mike's tearing eyes and quickly added, "and he probably is, but let her be for now. That stuff has hit her hard! She'll be out cold shortly which for her will be a blessing; at least she'll get some rest." Mike nodded and walked across the room to the table where he sat staring out at the snow falling relentlessly while Gerry tried again to reach the hospital.

Shaun lay motionless at the bottom of the pit. All around him were the children who, like him were trapped in this hellish existence. But unlike Shaun, they were hardened to the relentless routine of their existences, and the monsters that watched over them. Some older kids who were halfway to becoming monsters themselves laughed at the pale, still body that lay across the cold stone slabs. A door opened at the far end of the area, a sign that their work was finished for the day and they all stood in line to await the arrival of their keepers.

One small boy, curious to get a closer look at Shaun, ventured over to where he lay and stood over him peering at his face. He looked over his shoulder to check that he was not being observed before prodding Shaun's face with his finger. The moment he made contact with the pink soft skin the boy was suddenly propelled through the air by a powerful unseen force and went crashing into the garnet wall opposite. He screamed with the pain of contact and the burning sensation that ran through his arm.

"The white ones have him!" he screamed, as he fell to the ground. Suddenly all the children made a dash for the open door but were stopped by the keepers who had appeared at the entrance.

"What is this you say?" one of the monsters snarled through its teeth. The terrified boy scrambled to his feet and tried to scurry towards the door where the other children waited, but the monster barred his way with a large whip. As it looked at the boy it repeated the words, "What is this you say of the white ones?" Its voice was low and threatening.

The boy stood trembling for some time before managing to say, "I was wrong," he stammered. "He bit me on the finger!" he lied, as he looked fearfully up into the monster's blood red eyes. "I thought his soul was in transition but he is alive!"

"Get out of my way!" said the keeper as he pushed past the boy sending him sprawling onto the ground. As it stood gazing at Shaun he too made a gesture to prod him but was stopped short by the yell from the platform above.

"Leave him!" screamed the Sheelka soldier. The keeper moved away from Shaun's body and quickly motioned to the others to vacate the area. The fiend from Gohan, using its tail for support, climbed down to where Shaun lay and looked at his still face. Its huge tail slashed against the ground and it threw its head back in rage as it let out a roar like a crazed bull. Suddenly it took off from the ground, ascending high up into the air, and landed once again on the platform. Its snout ran with mucus, and saliva spurted from its mouth as enraged, it ordered the soldiers to take Shaun to Gohan. Two of the soldiers jumped from the platform, descending down through the murky air before coming to a stop by the side of Shaun's body.

Andy watched fascinated at the supernatural power of these beasts that, in spite of their proportions, could fly through the air like birds. Suddenly Andy was swept off the platform like a rag doll as one of the soldiers picked him up by the threads of his shirt, its talons digging into the flesh of his back. It stood for what seemed like agonising minutes and drew Andy closer to its face. He squirmed frantically in an effort to ease the pain from the Sheelka's grip and he turned his head away from its face to avoid the stench from its breath.

The soldier held him firmly in its grip as it looked intently into his fearful eyes, "You will now see Hell in all it's glory!" it said releasing its grip, sending Andy falling back down onto the platform. They walked through the door that the Gohan creature had entered onto the platform from earlier and Andy knew that whatever had come before, he was now being taken to a new level in terror. Once the door closed shut behind them, a resigned finality hit him like a bolt of lightening reminding him of the first time he was taken to prison. The pale yellow light that surrounded them highlighted the circular corridor, which resembled a spiral staircase in the turret of an old castle that he and Anna had once visited. He could see her in his mind's eye as they made their way along the circular corridor that had a steep gradient running downwards and he longed to be free of this place with its demons, monsters and stench.

Her last words to him echoed around inside his head warning him to clean up his act and get his life back. As he walked along between the two abominations that were taking him to Gohan he suddenly fell to his knees and screamed out his regret. He bent his body forward until his forearms rested on the floor in front of him and then he dropped his head onto his knees and found the tears that had escaped him in his cell back in The Place of Unrest.

The Sheelka soldiers both stopped short and gazed at the crying man rocking back and forth in his despair on the ground between them. The soldier that had been leading the way picked Andy up from the floor and held him close to its face, concentrating on the tears streaming down his cheeks and dripping off the end of his chin. In a fit of rage it threw him against the wall; and just as he struggled to his feet the other soldier descended on him like an enraged animal. It swiped its talons across his chest, sending him reeling backwards and as he jumped up defiantly they laughed at his attempts to fight them. One Sheelka made a move towards him once again but was stopped by the other soldier.

"Leave him," it said, "he is resisting the transition of his soul, look at his tears!" it said, pointing to Andy's face.

The Sheelka bent its head back and sniffed the air; "The white ones have found a way in." it said.

The other soldier snarled like an animal, "It's not possible; they cannot penetrate the forces of hell without losing their souls to us. No, they have not found a way in; this mortal has regret, which shows a softening of his human heart. But once he arrives in Gohan, that heart will harden and his true hatred will shine like a glowing ember and his heart will turn to stone."

The two soldiers watched Andy as he crouched on the stone floor that was now wet with his tears. As he gasped for breath between his sobs, he suddenly threw his arms open wide and screamed: "Lord, forgive me my sins and cleanse my soul so that I can save the boy before I am lost forever ..."

As he prayed, the Sheelka laughed at his words and mimicked him in his despair. Deep in the bowls of Gohan however, his prayers were heard by the six protectors of the pit ... known as Kassads. These beasts are the result of Satan's extreme desire to rule the world. Born of animal and demon they are guardians of hell. Their greatest quality is their shape-changing abilities which enable them to pass from one world to the next posing as political leaders, religious fanatics and corporate directors throughout the world. Their very existence is dependant upon the extent of mayhem and destruction they create and their rewards are spread over the face of the earth in death and violence. They invade their victim's body and mind and can alter history in just twenty-four hours, creating dictators so consumed with hatred that nations rise against nations and husband against wife, and child against child. Once their work on earth is complete they

Diane Marshall

return to hell triumphant in the knowledge that mayhem follows, bringing earth and hell closer to becoming a united world. Their true manifestation in hell is the genetic result of the creation of parent beings that are half demon and half animal. The product of these unnatural conceptions between these lower forms of beings called Assas and Dasks created the Kassads; ruthless flesh-eating monsters and harbourers of the blackest souls in hell.

Back in the passageway Andy heard a screech that resembled the cry of a tortured bird from farther along the corridor. The Sheelka soldiers let go of his arms and stood perfectly still, and he knew by their reaction that whatever was coming … was pure evil. A few seconds later a huge shadow spread itself across the floor where Andy lay, still face down, he could feel the rush of air from the flapping wings of the creature that hovered above him. Afraid to look he lay paralysed with fear feeling the icy tingle of terror creeping up his spine. The creature let out another screech that was almost deafening and Andy clasped his hands against his ears in an effort to shut out the hideous noise.

The Kassad swooped down from the yellow tinted air above, and came to land close by Andy's head. His eyes closed tight, and with a feeling of impending doom the terrified man summoned every inch of courage that he had left and slowly opened his eyes. The first thing he saw were the creature's huge paws that were it's feet, supporting strong legs that were covered in coarse hair and looked like the hind legs of a wolf. His fearful gaze

146

travelled higher until he saw the true horror in its entirety ... a beast manifested from all the nightmares of an entire army. A killing machine with no soul, it moved its face closer to him, its yellow eyes travelling the length of Andy's body, its grotesque mouth dripping salivary droplets onto its chest that was bare of hair and the only part of it that resembled anything human. The rest of it was a terrifying force of supernatural embodiment that once looked upon, would surely taint the soul of Christ himself. Andy could feel its power spreading through his body like a rushing tide surging through every vein and seeping out through every pore.

As he gazed upon the Kassad, taking in every detail of the features of its face, he felt his soul grasping at the hideous vision, like a man gulping fresh water after being lost in a desert for days. The yellow eyes twinkled with menace as they gazed upon the mortal who thought he was a big shot on earth; he had so much to learn.

The face of the Kassad grinned, exposing black teeth from its bear-like jaws, its ears like those of a proud dog's, sitting high on its head, moved in a twitching motion as it listened to the final screeching of this mortal's soul as the very last drop of goodness left it. Andy could feel the tremendous power gushing through him like an explosion and all fear left him. He stood up and faced the Kassad with a feeling of equality and an evil menace inside him that was eager to escape.

Mike and Gerry quietly left Jan to sleep off the brandy and headed out of the room and along the narrow passageway. The smell of hot broth welcomed them, lifting their depleted spirits momentarily. Just as they reached the top of the stairs the electricity finally gave up, plunging the small inn into complete darkness. They stood perfectly still for a few seconds while their eyes adjusted to the gloom. Their hearts raced as the chatter they had heard from the floor below stopped, and was replaced by an unnerving silence. They stood for what seemed like an age in the cold passageway before the glow of candlelight illuminated the bottom of the stairs and the rumble of chatter started up again.

Once they were in the bar, Mike took a few candles and made his way back up to the room. Jan was still out cold, and he lit three candles and left them standing on the table, before once again making his way down to the bar. An urn of soup had been placed on the bar with large mugs and thickly cut loaves of bread. A surprisingly orderly group of people were already standing in line awaiting their turn to scoop out the hot meal and return to their seats, some sitting on the floor. Gerry's voice rang out over the chatter and summoned Mike to a darkened corner opposite the fireplace where he offered his friend a steaming mug of broth. The two men stood in silence for a few moments each lost in their own thoughts. A woman standing by the entrance to the bar let out a startled scream and forced her way through the crowd and clung onto a large man standing near the fireplace. Bewildered at her outburst, the occupants of the bar stared at her for a few seconds before they saw what had frightened her. A priest stumbled into the room holding a bible. His hands were covered in blood and the expression on his face was one of horror.

"We are all doomed!" he said without raising his voice, "Satan is here, he has come, as he promised he would." The next instant the priest's entire body burst into flames and his blood curdling screams sent most of the occupants in the bar scurrying towards the main entrance to the guest house, and out onto the street. Mike and Gerry made for the stairs striding them two at a time in their haste to get to Jan.

Dougie the inn's proprietor, together with his wife Kate, blasted the priest's body with fire extinguishers. Then to their horror, the burning body rose from the floor and turned upside down. The charred arms spread out from his sides, and the whole mass resembled a flaming inverted cross. The rest of the people left in the bar fled out into the freezing night.

Upstairs, Mike found his wife awake but groggy, and thankfully, oblivious to the horrific scene downstairs. More screams from downstairs sent Gerry hurrying back down to the bar as Mike tried to comfort Jan who was now very much awake and even more frightened than before. She buried her face into her husband's chest eager to know what was going on, but afraid to ask.

When Gerry ran into the bar he saw the charred remains of the priest lying on the floor. Nothing remained of the once human form, no sign of bones, teeth or even the gold crucifix he had worn around his neck, all that was left was a pile of ash. There was complete silence in the bar as the proprietor, and his wife and daughter Vivian stared in disbelief at the remains of the priest. Finally, Dougie ran into the hallway and quickly secured the entrance door. Mike and Jan waited at the bottom of the stairs whilst Gerry tried to comfort the two women.

Dougie's face was ashen when he returned from the hallway and he bypassed his wife and daughter who stood trembling, clinging on tightly to each other unable to tear their eyes away from the remains of the priest. When he reached Gerry he grabbed both his arms and dragged him to the far corner of the bar. With his voice trembling and tears shimmering in his eyes, he said, "God help me, for I've either gone insane or those things I just saw out there are real."

The fear that swept through Gerry threatened to paralyze his legs and he grabbed Dougie by the shoulders. "What did you see?" he demanded.

The terrified man broke free from his grip and scurried around to the other side of the bar, where he poured two whiskies and handing one to Gerry, he said; "You'd better drink that first." A blood curdling scream from outside snapped Dougie out of his shock.

"Move!" he screamed as he ran from behind the bar. Nobody hung around to ask any questions as they all followed him upstairs. On the top landing they waited in front of a locked door as Dougie fumbled in his pocket for the key. Outside, they could hear people screaming and a loud clatter against the downstairs main door made him more terrified as he tried frantically to find the keys. Finally, Gerry put his hands on the terrified man's shoulders and gently shook him; the fear in his eyes sent an icy tingle up his spine.

"Are you sure you didn't leave the key in the bar?" he asked. It was Kate who stepped forward and reached into her husband's pocket and retrieved the set of keys hidden under his wallet. Dougie suddenly took over the situation once again and unlocked the door, behind which lay another set of stairs. Once again they followed him, each glancing back, for fear that whatever was out there may have penetrated the main outside door. Once this door was unlocked, everyone huddled just inside the room in complete silence as the darkness hung heavy like a cold thick fog penetrating through to their bones. Kate and Vivian felt their way into the room and found some candles, and soon the whole room flickered into life in a soft glow yellow glow. Dougie made his way to a calor gas stove that sat in the centre of a small kitchen on the left of the room. He lit all four burners and beckoned everyone to sit at a table opposite the stove. The room was a large attic that ran the length of the building. It had a fully fitted living, sleeping and eating area, and had it not been for the extraordinary circumstances, it would have been a cosy, pleasant place to spend time in.

Kate busied herself making tea whilst Vivian fetched blankets that were gratefully received for the attic was icy cold. Dougie joined the others at the table, and there was a curious silence as Kate put a large pot of tea, sugar, milk and mugs in the centre of the table. Gerry motioned toward Dougie to join him over by the two large sofas as he made his up from his seat.

"You would be as well staying where you are." said Dougie as he looked thoughtfully at the frightened faces around the table. "We all have to know what's out there." he said with a slight tremble to his voice. He put his elbows on the table and held his head in his hands, his fingers curling, sending his nails digging into his head. He looked up and finally said "There are unnatural beasts pulling people under the drifts and it's so deep that you can't see how they kill them, for all that's left are the crimson stains in the snow.

"What beasts? What are you talking about?" asked his wife whose face had taken on a grey hue.

He left his seat and walked round the table where he knelt by the side of her chair, and taking her hand in his he said; "They're out of hell! It's as the priest said, they're out of hell!"

CHAPTER ELEVEN

———◆———

Back in room 11, Anna and Mia waited anxiously for Nurse Scott's return.

"I don't think she's coming back!" Anna whispered before turning and throwing herself into Mia's arms, clinging tightly to her friend, she was afraid to let go.

"My God! You're shaking uncontrollably." cried Mia, who was herself feeling more frightened than she appeared. "Let's get you off your feet before your legs give way altogether."

She led the white-faced Anna across the room to one of the vacant beds; "Lie down here for a while." she said, and Anna obeyed without question pulling the duvet up tight against her chin. Alison suddenly screamed out and sat up struggling to get out of bed. Mia ran to comfort her, whispering quietly to the child, her words seeming to calm her. She slipped into the bed beside the frightened child and held her close whilst stroking her hair, and soon she was calm once again. Meanwhile, Anna had jumped out of bed and was slowly making her way to the door.

"Did you hear that?" she said, turning toward Mia.

"What?" she questioned.

"There was someone tapping on the door." Anna replied. Just then, the tapping was unmistakable.

"Don't open the door!" cried Mia, but her plea seemed to fall on deaf ears as Anna slowly inched her way to the door. Another tap sounded, followed by the sound of a child's voice calling for Nurse Emma. Anna immediately opened the door to find a little boy of about two years of age standing in the passageway. Anna's fear melted as she looked at the child's tear-stained face.

"I want to see my mummy." he cried, as he held up his arms needing to be picked up and comforted. Anna swept him into her arms and took him into the room and sat on the bed with him on her lap and gently rocked him.

"It's all right sweetheart," she soothed, "Nurse Emma will be here soon.

Mia had gotten up and joined them on the bed; "Poor little thing." she said, whilst running her fingers through the child's blond curls. "How on earth did he get out of the children's ward?" she said.

"I can't imagine." said Anna … adding "I thought all the doors were locked. Just then the child started to cough, his little hands clung onto his chest and his face contorted in pain. Anna stood up and held the child against her shoulder and tried patting his back, but the coughing seemed to get worse. Glancing at the door Anna knew that she would have to take the child back along the corridor to his own ward if he didn't improve.

Mia went to the bedside cabinet and poured a little water into a plastic cup, but when she returned the child had gone limp in Anna's arms. "Oh my God we have to get him back!" she cried.

Anna nodded and made for the door, fearful of not getting him there in time for whatever help he needed. She unlocked the door once again and hastily stepped into the gloomy passageway, holding the child close to her breast and in an instant she was gone.

Mia stood for a few seconds trying to see through the small glass panel into the corridor but it was too dark on the other side. The emergency lights flickered ominously, and the thought of the room being plunged into complete darkness was enough to send her hurrying back to bed with her child held close.

Anna had turned left along the corridor toward the children's ward, the child still limp in her arms moaned softly. She slowed her pace as she became aware of footsteps behind her, ahead all was quiet, too quiet. Instinctively drawing the child closer she stopped walking and stood perfectly still, the hairs on the back of her neck stood on end. She was petrified as she suddenly rushed forward, desperate to reach the ward.

When a voice from behind her called out, "Just a moment young lady!" she turned to see two Doctors hurrying along the corridor. Her relief was so intense that she almost let go of the child.

"Here let me take him." said the younger looking doctor. "How long have you been wandering around here?" he added. "We saw this little boy outside of our room and he appeared to be lost and looking for Nurse Emma …"

"Never mind that just now." he interrupted "I'll take the child and I'm sure Doctor Forbes will look after you." he said as he walked away.

"He will be all right won't he?" she turned to the doctor with anxious eyes. "I've every reason to think so my dear, little Tommy's been with us for quite some time and his seizures are well known to us. But, what I'd like to know is why are you still on this floor?"

"I'm not sure I understand …Why shouldn't we be here?"

Doctor Forbes was incredulous. "My dear young woman, this floor has been evacuated! Part of the south tower has given way under the weight of the snow."

"Oh my God; we better get Mia!" cried Anna, but as she made to go back to room 11 the doctor grabbed hold of her arm.

"Security is on their way up here to make sure that everyone has been taken to safety, and it's just as well by the sound of it. Hurry, this way." he said as he pulled Anna along the corridor in the opposite direction to room 11.

"Are you sure they'll get her and her child out?" "I can bet my reputation on it; now let's get a move on."

They ran along the corridor until they reached a central area that had four passageways running off it.

156

Doctor Forbes hesitated for a moment before turning left where they came across an elevator.

"This'll do." he said as he pressed the down button.

"Where are we going?" asked Anna.

"To the outpatients department." the doctor replied without looking at her.

"What's really going on here?" she asked as they waited nervously for the lift, but before he could answer her question, the lift doors swept open. Once inside Anna noticed that the doctor pressed the button for the basement.

"I thought the outpatients department was on the ground floor." she said without looking at Doctor Forbes.

"It is," he replied, "but that's not where you're going."

Anna felt herself breaking out into a cold sweat: "Look I don't know about you but I'm going to the outpatients department with the rest of the evacuees." Before she could say any more, the lift doors opened making the familiar sweeping noise that only moments before had seemed to be a source of comfort, but now it registered a sickening sound that reverberated inside her head.

With her pulse racing and icy fingers curling their way up her spine she stood shaking, unable to move. Behind her there came a blood curdling laugh and then she was pushed out of the lift into the dank corridor. She looked back and the scream died in her throat as she looked into the eyes of a Kassad.

"Die well, mortal!" it growled as the lift doors closed. Alone in the corridor she gasped for breath for her lungs seemed to have shut down. She tried to move but her feet felt like they were made of lead. Ahead in the distance she heard the laughter of a child, but she knew that no mortal child could ever laugh in such a guttural way. From out of the gloom appeared the little boy that she had held so close to her breast only minutes before. As he glided towards her, seemingly on invisible wheels, she tried to run but as in a nightmare, her legs would not move. He floated into the air and hovered above her and the last thing she saw before the darkness claimed her were his blackened teeth as he opened his mouth wide and laughed.

Back in the bowels of hell, Andy sat by the side of a huge onyx doorway and as it clicked open he instinctively knew that he belonged beyond it. As he walked into the secret chamber that all black souls sought he cried out fearfully, as he became aware that he was floating in black space.

Up ahead the entire planet earth rolled in front of him at an incredible speed suspended in the blackness. As each country of the world flashed before him his mind was bombarded with the knowledge of Satan's secret agencies hard at work organising their destruction. London, Paris, Rome, Hong Kong, New York, and Russia all flashed before him. Unnatural storms raged throughout the planet. Seas rose up like demons before descending upon their helpless prey, and snow storms immobilised entire countries. And as hell's plans were revealed to him he understood the reasons behind the raging war.

The child named Wendy, together with the boy Shaun were God's own creations destined to save the world. Together they would become protectors of the entire planet and as the centuries passed there would engage vast armies of followers in their quest for the perfect world.

As each new soul is formed in the Hall of Dawn in heaven's Kingdom, the glowing tiny orb is passed through the hands of God himself for his blessing before making its journey earth bound. The soul then passes to the uterus of the earth mother through the guidance of the Angels of Providence.

In the case of Wendy, her soul was infused with a single tear from the eye of God as it passed through his hand. So sad was he, that he cried for the souls he was sending to join the population on earth, where all manner of evil awaited. Filled with the essence of God, the girl's soul glowed brighter than any other. And so it was decreed that she descend to her earth mother for her first incarnation one thousand years ago. Since then she has lived many lives on earth to enable her to truly understand the nature of man and woman alike. Her faith has grown stronger with every life lived, and she has grown to possess wisdom that far exceeds any other mortal. And now, her present incarnation has ended and she will journey to the Hall of Truth in the Kingdom of Heaven and there she will learn her fate. After one thousand years of incarnations she will become immortal therefore destroying Satan's plan to rule Heaven, Hell and Earth. The critical time is nearing as the end of her millennium draws near, for if she is immortalised then Satan's army will face defeat. The portal has opened at the place of her first incarnation one thousand years ago in a back room of a small farmhouse. Since then many structures have stood on that spot until finally, the hospital that the child would die in.

But now there were only two hours left before the portal closed for another thousand years. Before then, the child must be taken through the portal holding the hand of one she trusts so that her mortal body dies in hell. Her soul would be captured by all the dark forces in Hell's power assuring her ruination so that she would never survive anywhere but in Hell itself leaving Satan assured of world domination.

The boy destined to stand by her side was already safe in the bowels of Gohan. His soul that over the years has had intimate knowledge of hers is growing dimmer with every passing minute and the progression of their journey together, being reincarnated only to unite with each other as higher beings on earth is all but over. God's own Angels dare not enter Hell's corridors for their pure souls would be so overcome by the dark forces that they would be destroyed for all eternity. World domination, riches beyond imagination and the defeat of the one who cast him out of Heaven was Satan's driving force, and he would not be satisfied until the King of Angels bowed at his feet.

After this revelation, Andy found himself once again sitting by the side of the great onyx door, but unknown to him, the whole truth had not been revealed. Mordrand had followed Zeenkell, who was in the guise of Doctor

McGregor, to the basement of the hospital. Many of the side rooms along the corridor were filled with patients and staff all under the impression that they would soon be led to safety.

"Ah, all the little lambs soon to be led to the slaughter." said the dark angel derisively as soon as he was aware of Mordrand's presence behind him.

"They will not die in Hell." said Mordrand, as the two powers faced each other in the dim corridor.

Zeenkell lunged toward Mordrand, grabbed him by the throat and threw him along the corridor. As he landed on the floor the Angel from Hell flew through the air on black wings and descended upon him. Grabbing him with clawed feet he swept him up from the ground and held him suspended in the murky air. Mordrand twisted his body free and swung around, his own wings flapping golden white. Circling each other like opponents in a boxing ring, they stared into each others eyes, each defying the other to make a move. Swiftly Mordrand's hand tore at Zeenkell's belly spilling blood as black as coal onto the floor below. The dark Angel screamed out but not with pain; he screamed in abhorrence that a white Angel had punctured his flesh and ripped his bowel. The physical damage was of no consequence, but the fact that a Heavenly Being had touched the inside of his flesh was dangerous.

CHAPTER TWELVE

———◆———

Anna regained consciousness on the floor of the basement outside the lift. Her head felt heavy and the stench in the air was nauseating. She stood up on unsteady legs and toyed with the idea of pressing the button on the side panel next to the lift, but the memory of the beast that had stood inside it sent her scurrying along the corridor in search of the stairs. Catching her breath, she stopped and steadied herself by placing the palms of her hands against the dirty wall. She froze for a few seconds as an unearthly screeching echoed through the corridor. Turning, she pressed her back tight up against the wall and forced herself to look in the direction of the noise. Out of the murkiness she saw two winged beings locked in combat flying along the corridor. Screaming, she started to run along the dim passageway, feeling her way along the wall.

The awful screeching was now directly above her and the frantic flapping of their wings stirred the air around her, twisting and swirling her hair in its wake.

Her shaking hands found an indent in the wall, and to her relief she discovered that it was a door frame. It seemed like an eternity until her fumbling hands finally located a metal lever, and to her immense surprise it opened the door. She quickly darted inside, relieved to shut out the sight and sound of the feuding pair.

The Kassad, in the guise of Mr Hillman, the hospital's eminent brain surgeon, hovered outside room 11. As he gazed at the mother lying in bed with her sleeping child on her breast, he decided that Alison would be the one to take Wendy through the portal. So intent was he contemplating his next move that he was quite unaware that the Angel Azearna was standing behind him. After a few moments had passed he suddenly sensed her presence and slowly turned around.

"I thought I could smell the scent of a bitch." he said, glaring at her through blood red eyes.

"This is not the child you seek." said the Angel.

"You know nothing of my plans," he hissed, "and I would have thought that you would have scurried along to sit by the feet of your God by now, for you have very little time left."

He opened his mouth wide and laughed. "Perhaps you could wash the blood of all his little Angels from his hands, for he alone is responsible for the destruction of your Heavenly Kingdom. Tell me Angel … how does it feel to know that he has lied to you from the very beginning of time?"

Azearna smiled. "You know nothing of my God, Kassad, for his plans unfold as we speak, ensuring that the child will never see your repugnant world."

Enraged the Kassad grabbed Azearna by her throat and lifted her off her feet. "What has he ever done for you? Other than to send you here to spend your last minutes on earth suspended above the head of a Kassad. What has he ever given you Angel?"

In answer to his question, Azearna slowly traced her finger down the centre of her chest, and as she did so the flesh opened, revealing a heart that with every beat grew brighter … "He gave me this." she said.

Unable to look upon her any longer, the Kassad let go of her and fled screaming in pain as his eyes burned from the sight of purity.

Clare stood by the side of Wendy's bed and listened in wonder as Shrancanna spoke to the child. "Little one," she said, "the time has come for you to prepare for your very special journey."

"Can Clare come too?" asked the child. The Angel sat on the edge of Wendy's bed and took hold of her small hand

"Do you remember when we spoke about going to visit with your mother in Heaven, Wendy?" The child nodded and Shrancanna whispered, "I will be with you …"

Clare choked back a tear and looked pleadingly at the Angel, and as if she read her thoughts Shrancanna smiled before saying, "She is not going to die, she is going to learn about her future, and once there, she will remember her past."

A nurse hurried to the side of the bed and whispered into the Angel's ear and without saying another word, Shrancanna picked the child up, and swiftly made her way to a side room within the ward.

"You must not cry for the child, Clare." said the nurse. "Now we must get Mia and Alison, they will be safer in here. There is an invisible force binding the doors and windows making it impossible for the dark ones to enter. They can only do so if invited so remember, do not answer the door to anyone even if you recognise them, for the dark ones are masters of disguise. All the children here will sleep until all is quiet once more."

Without saying any more she was joined by two other nurses, and together they left the ward.

Anna found a bolt behind the door in the basement and quickly drew it home securing it tightly. She moved forward cautiously and discovered that there was another door at the end of the narrow L-shaped passageway. She pressed her ear tight against it until she was satisfied that the coast was clear. Holding her breath, she slowly pushed the lever down and warily opened the door a few inches and to her surprise she saw streaks of light shining through a window opposite her. She moved closer, and as her eyes became accustomed to the light she realised that the window was the top half of another door. Cautiously, she peered into the area through the glass and was relieved to find a very ordinary looking office. The small square room was furnished with a desk that sat to the left of another door, and opposite to that stood a filing cabinet with the top drawer left open. Two easy chairs sat in the middle of the room, one with a magazine resting on top of a scatter cushion. The seat behind the desk was pulled back as though the person who vacated it left in a hurry.

Her heart beat wildly as she entered the office and found herself standing on grey cord carpet. Her eyes scanned the desktop that was littered with blue coloured forms that read 'Interim Notification of Death' printed in bold black letters. Next to these were Post-Mortem notes and a Death Certificate booklet, and placed in the centre of the desk was a large register. To the side of the wooden desk sat a small cabinet with a computer on top of it; the screen was flashing a message that read, 'The dead will conquer.'

Terrified she almost ran through the door that would have led her back into the dark basement corridor, but the memory of the creature stayed her. She stood with her back against the door, with her hand pressed tight against her mouth for fear that she would scream out.

Breathing heavily through her nostrils, her eyes darting in every direction, she was well aware that she was in a Mortuary office. A sudden thought sprang into her mind … the dead have to be taken to the undertaker's parlours; there must be a way out from here!

She made her way to the door by the side of the desk and with trembling hands she twisted the knob clockwise, it made a clicking noise and swung open. She hesitated for a few seconds, her heartbeat sounding in her ears as she peered into the room beyond. Facing her were rows of cabinets with smaller inlaid stainless steel doors that stretched along the entire length of the wall. There were three sets of doors per cabinet, one at the top, one in the middle and one that sat about twelve inches from the cold terrazzo floor. There were white marker boards on each door, some with names that had been written with a black marker pen while others remained blank. There was the constant drone of machinery humming and clicking, as the body fridges re-set their temperatures and there was a strong smell of disinfectant that hung heavily in the air. A small wash handbasin stood in the centre of the adjacent wall and next to it stood a large white laundry bag that was hooked onto a wheeled metal frame. Next to that were a set of double swing doors with opaque glass windows. Along the opposite wall was a large hydraulic body hoist that had an electric cable running from the handle bar into a battery charger that sat close by on the floor. Above this sat a wall-mounted telephone right next to a large set of double doors.

Anna summoned all her courage and entered the room and headed straight for the doors. She turned the yale and drew back three large bolts and pushed the door but it would not budge; trying again and again she could not move the door for the weight of the snow lying against it. Eventually, she gave up and kicked the door in frustration.

She stood for what seemed like an age, trying to decide on her next move when she heard a tapping noise.

Frozen with fear, she tried to determine where the noise was coming from … the tapping sounded again and this time she knew that it was coming from one of the body fridges. Terrified she leaped across the room in seconds and ran straight through the glass panelled doors and out into a small changing area. Halfway along the wall facing her were rows of lockers and in the corner next to them sat rows of white theatre boots neatly positioned on a wooden slatted frame. On shelves above these were neatly folded blue theatre tunics, pants and green plastic aprons. To her right were three shower units, one with the plastic curtain drawn fully across and she could hear water dripping. The only other sound she could hear was her own heavy breathing.

She saw a door to the left of the changing area, next to a pile of white towels and a laundry buggy. Slowly, she inched her way farther into the room and as she glanced back at the shower she saw the curtain move. Screaming she ran through the door and plunged into a square tiled pool filled with milky fluid. Panic stricken, she scrambled around frantically trying to get to get to her feet. Her eyes stung, and the strong odour of disinfectant caught in the back of her throat, and when she finally crawled out she lay on the cold tiled floor. She sat shivering for a few moments whilst her eyes cleared, and   realised that she had fallen into a disinfectant pit of only about ten inches deep.

She stood up and looked around the square room and saw that she was in some sort of surgical theatre. In the middle of the area sat four stainless steel slabs that were supported by cylinder structures made of the same shiny material. Hanging on a metal hook around the cylinder was a shower hose that looked to be retractable. There were numerous white metal glass cabinets against a wall each filled with sharp knives, scalpels, metal T-Bars, saws, forceps, scissors and white buckets each with labels attached. On the opposite wall stood two huge stainless steel sinks with hosepipes attached to the taps and they were set in large stainless steel worktops and sitting on top of them were two white plastic chopping boards. At the back of the sinks was a large window that that looked into a small viewing area with four seats with microphones hanging down from the ceiling and positioned above them.

With her arms crossed over in front of her chest and her fingers grasping tightly into her upper arms, she slowly made her way farther into the room. There was an acrid stench that hung in the air like a cloud and she felt a burning need to get out of there quickly. She made her way past three of the slabs but as she neared the fourth, near an exit door, she slowed her pace, for she could see the outline of a body lying there. As she gingerly neared it, the repugnant odour hit her like a slap on the face and on the slab lay a body that had been cut open. The y-shaped incision ran from each side of the neck and all the way down the mid-line of the body before stopping just short of the pubic bone.

The sight shocked her so badly that she could do nothing but stop, and stare at what was left of the man lying there. There was a wooden block wedged under the waxy shoulders, and the head was hanging back but not touching the slab. The scalp had been pulled down over the front of his face, and the entire back of his head was missing. The sternum had been removed, exposing the heart and lungs. Beneath the diaphragm the stomach was bloated as though it were full of air, and the liver to the right of the cavity looked swollen, greasy and yellow. Two empty buckets were wedged between the feet of the body that was surrounded in yellow body fluid streaked with blood.

The shriek that eventually escaped from her echoed around the room and resembled that of a tormented animal and she ran past the slab and through yet another door. She found herself in what appeared to be a waiting room and she stood there with one hand across her mouth, and the other clutching the neck of her sweater close to her throat. Behind her she could hear squelching noises coming from behind the door. She looked through a small single glass panel on the door and again she found herself staring at a Kassad, but he was too busy eating the organs of the body on the slab to notice her.

Just as her legs gave way, she was swept up into the air by one of the winged beings she had seen earlier in the corridor. Semi-conscious, she looked into the eyes of Mordrand and she threw her arm around his neck and clung tightly to him.

Chapter Thirteen

The cots in the children's ward had been arranged in a circle at the far end next to the nurse's office and sitting in the middle of them was an Angel, with its wings wrapped around it and head bowed as if in silent prayer. Outside, the corridor bore the consequences of the battle and there were black and white feathers littered over the floor, many soaked in blood.

Wendy sat cradled in the arms of Shrancanna as they flew above the clouds that looked like cotton candy. Everything was bright, but not overbearing as they soared through violet, pink and yellow hues. Eventually they came to a stop and gently swayed as though they were floating in a warm calm sea.

The child was fascinated as complete silence engulfed them, wrapping around them like silk. And to her amazement, there was no floor, ceiling, beginning or end to this incredible place. She thought of the rainbow on the cover of her favourite story book and she truly felt that there really was treasure at the end of it.

When they suddenly stopped, the child wondered if they had reached their destination.

As though reading her thoughts, Shrancanna smiled down on the child and said, "We are in the waiting place, and here we must remain until we are admitted into The Hall of Truth."

Just as she finished speaking, a pink shimmering glow appeared off in the distance. As it moved closer, its shape took on a more solid appearance and when it finally stopped in front of them the child felt afraid. The shape drew closer still and shifted into a huge vertical strip of pink light. All at once the strip widened and opened up like the doors of an elevator all the while moving closer until they were completely engulfed by the light. The silence of earlier was broken, and in its place there was the sound of a slow running river. As the pink light faded, they found themselves standing on plush soft grass, and off in the distance appeared a narrow stream. Just as though an artist's brush were painting in the scenery, there emerged rolling hills off in the distance and at the foot of these there appeared a crystal palace.

"It's magic!" cried the child excitedly.

The Angel laughed softly. "It's not magic Wendy;" she said, "its truth!" Shrancanna set the child down onto the grass that felt warm under her bare feet.

"We must walk along by the side of the river." she told the child. who happily placed her hand in Shrancanna's as they set off. As they began to walk along the bank the child realised that this was no ordinary river, for as she looked through the crystal clear water she could see the world, as the river flowed through the ages of time.

"This is the River of Life, child" said the Angel, pausing to smile at the wonder on Wendy's face before continuing, "From the very beginning of time when God created the earth, his greatest desire for the human race was for them to live in peace and harmony. Not only loving each other but also loving the earth that was created for them. Through the ages, man has become so corrupt that the earth and all its inhabitants are in grave danger. The dark Angel Satan and his followers are now at war with Heaven in a bid to rule the earth and we must stop him."

"But how?" asked the child "The answer lies here in the river of life, little one." said Shrancanna, pointing down toward the river. "As we walk by the side of the river you will see that every moment in time has been recorded. At the end of the river, the water runs into a vast lake called The Lake of Tranquillity. There, many of heaven's Higher Angels gather together to discuss the state of the world, and how best to bring comfort and hope to its earthly beings. For many years now, it has not been easy for them to see the true nature of the world, for the Lake grows darker as man's sins on earth multiply. Now the situation has become critical, for the Lake has lost its tranquillity and roars with anger like a mighty sea in a violent storm. Without the Lake's calm the Higher Angels cannot assist the earth, and that means that all humanity walks the earth without their Guardian Angels by their sides and without them, they are left vulnerable to the dark forces."

As the child listened to Shrancanna, her mind expanded and memories of her past lives started to float through doors that are closed to earth-bound mortals.

"I know this place." she said in a way that belied her earth years and the Angel responded with a knowing smile.

As they walked on Shrancanna added, "Although the Higher Angels have never lived on earth, their knowledge of mankind is exceptional for they understand the true nature of mortals. Look into the water, child, and you will see that there are shallow parts with small rocks, some of which sit higher than the water level." Wendy knelt down by the side of the river and gazed intently into the water. "In life all mortals face trials and tribulations throughout their time on earth, many times their situations become so extreme that they give up. When mortals lose hope the dark forces have an open invitation to creep into their souls and that turns them away from all that is good, and their souls are lost forever. These rocks in the river represent rescue from drowning in the sea of humanity. The Higher Angels study the Lake of Tranquillity and guide the troubled souls onto the rocks where they reflect on their lives and from there are guided forward. These are the souls who learn from their earthly mistakes and so the learning process moves them closer to a greater understanding of life. Eventually, they become wiser, therefore able to move forward through their earthly lives without help from The Higher Ones. When their earthly years are over and they return once again to their home here in Heaven, a review of their time on earth takes place. Once that has been considered, they are then enlightened so that they realise how far they have travelled in their quest for spiritual awareness. Many of them choose to return to earth so that they can learn from past mistakes. Some take many lifetimes on earth to realise their goals, whilst others may only take two or three. Those who need extra guidance will be counselled by the Higher Angels before their return to earth. Although they are born into the world as helpless infants, they remember as they grow what was taught to them by the Higher Ones, and human beings call this having a conscience. Now, let us walk on little one."

As they resumed their path along the riverside Shrancanna could see that there was a new depth to the child's eyes, and was satisfied that her enlightenment had begun. As they walked the child noticed that the water was no longer clear and she bent down to peer deeper into the river. There was undergrowth tangled around the rocks that had become green and slimy. Farther along, they passed the crystal palace that stood to their right and just behind it, the sky grew darker. The warm breeze of earlier suddenly vanished and was replaced by a cold wind, and above them were dark rolling clouds.

When they reached the lake, there was no sign of the clear tranquil water, for it was as black as coal and it tumbled and rolled angrily. Wendy, overwrought by the sight, fell to her knees and wept. Shrancanna let her be until her tears were spent before urging her to walk back the way they had come.

"You must enter the palace, Wendy." said Shrancanna. "From there you will visit your past, your present-day and your future. I will escort you as far as the second entrance but then you must enter by yourself."

They walked in silence toward the glistening building, and when they reached a huge arched door they waited. The door was made of the same material as the rest of the building and had intricately cut sculptures of haloed Angels covering every inch of the gleaming surface.

"Who are they?" asked Wendy.

"They are the Higher Angels." replied Shrancanna.

When the door opened it swung silently inward, and standing at each side of the entrance were two individuals dressed in pink robes. It was not possible to determine if they were male or female for their bodies were lean and completely covered in their robes. Both had short blond hair and bright blue eyes, and a hint of a smile played along their perfectly shaped lips. As Shrancanna and Wendy entered, the two beings bowed their heads slightly before stepping backward and disappearing into alcoves at each side of the door.

They walked along a wide passageway, on either side of which sat crystal columns with huge vases of flowers shining so brightly that they looked as if they too were fashioned from crystal. Beside these sat high-backed long sofas in a pale pink satin material, and in front of them stood intricately designed crystal tables, some of which had pale blue glass books sitting on top of them. As they passed, Wendy couldn't help wondering if the Haloed Angels sat upon them.

Eventually, they reached another huge arched door where Shrancanna knelt down in front of the child. Taking both of her hands in hers she said, "This is where I must leave you, but I will be here when you return."

As she stood up and turned to leave she whispered, "Do not be afraid."

But Wendy was afraid and when the great door opened she wanted to run into the Angel's arms for she did not want to enter this place alone. Two beings exactly like the others who stood at the outside door stood by the side of this entrance. One of them raised an arm indicating the direction in which she should follow, no words were spoken but when the being smiled warmly, the child felt a little better. As she entered this new area she could see nothing in front of her, for all that was evident was the crystal floor that she stood upon.

Suddenly as before, there appeared a semi-circular room as though some great artist painted it out in front of her. The room had arched windows all around it but there was no glass in them; instead billowing in a warm breeze hung pale blue and pink transparent curtains. To her left there appeared a balcony with a gleaming spiral balustrade around its semi-circular shape. The air carried the scent of roses, and in the distance she could hear the sound of birds sighing. She slowly walked out onto the balcony and peered through a space in the balustrade onto the beautiful scenery below where the river of life's water still ran clear. A movement to her right caused her to turn around, and standing by the side of a huge crystal vase of roses was a young woman.

"May I join you?" the woman asked the child who looked a little startled. Wendy nodded her head without speaking and the young woman slowly walked across the balcony. The child took in every detail as the woman moved closer. She was very pretty with green eyes and red hair that tumbled around her slim shoulders and she was dressed in a simple white full length dress. As she came to a stop in front of the child she knelt down and gazed lovingly into the small face that now held no hint of fear.

In a soft tone, the woman spoke to the child saying, "You have grown into a very pretty girl Wendy, and I have waited for this moment ever since you were born. All at once the child knew that she was standing in front of her mother and threw herself into her arms. As they kissed and hugged each other, their tears of joy mingling, another presence appeared on the balcony but this time she immediately recognised him. The man that she had known all of her earth life scooped her up in his arms and pressed her head against his chest.

"Daddy!" she cried and without any words being spoken between them, she instinctively knew that her adoptive father's life on earth had ended.

"We're running short of time." he said as he set the child down and took hold of her hand. Moments later all three silently walked to the right side of the balcony where they stopped in front of a door, but unlike the others, this door was transparent and beyond it, stood a glass spiral stairway. When the door opened silently they entered into this new area that had no visible floor but the firmness underfoot was reassuring.

Wendy knew that the rest of the journey was for her alone, and as she headed for the stairs she did not look back. The glass step felt warm under her bare feet and all fear dissipated, leaving in its place a reassurance that she was truly loved, safe and surrounded by a presence that she had known for centuries. In an instant, she found herself at the top of the stairway surrounded by a golden light so beautiful that she wanted to stay in its warm glow for all time. A warm fragrant mist swirled around her lifting her hair in its wake and just as the thought crossed her mind that she would like to see beyond it, the mist vanished.

When her eyes became accustomed to her new surroundings, she was aware that she was standing in a white room. It was not a large room; in fact it could have been any room in a well kept home on earth. There were pictures on the walls, a writing desk, and sofas with large plump cushions, occasional tables and glass doors that led out onto a spectacular garden. Outside, she could see a figure rising from a garden bench that was surrounded by roses. As she moved closer to the glass door she saw that this being was very tall, and was dressed in a pale pink glowing robe. She felt no fear as she watched her glide over the plush grass towards the door, and when it opened she could see a halo around her head. Her eyes shone like diamonds and her smile held the child captivated in its beauty and when she held out her hand, Wendy willingly took hold of it and together, they walked into the garden.

"We have been waiting anxiously for your return, child." she said, as they walked toward the garden bench where they both sat down. The Angel did not speak as she rested the flat of her hand on the child's chest.

Wendy instantly fell forward as she lost consciousnesses and was immediately taken from the bench and carried to a small glass dome. There she was laid on a pink oval shape silk bed, her head resting snugly on a soft pillow made of the same material, and as the Angel left the dome the structure closed, leaving the child alone inside.

From deep within her slumber, the child's soul awakened to the true nature of her past lives on earth. She saw herself surrounded by family as she gave birth to twins; a son and daughter whom she named Mordrand and Malleena respectively during her first incarnation, two thousand years ago.

Over the centuries she lived and died, having known all manner of sin, pride and greed. From her first incarnation through to the present day she gained a wealth of experience that was forever etched on her soul, and throughout her entire creation, her soul followed the path of its intended journey ... to this place in heaven to receive the knowledge of her being, together with the husband of her past lives and the children she bore him, for unlike any other offspring, theirs were eternal Angels.

Spread over the earth, her Angels were now fighting the forces of evil; denying the dark one's plan to rule the world. From every major city to the smallest of villages across the planet, Satan's presence was felt with all the horror that hell had to offer. Military fighter jets were grounded, helicopters spun like spinning tops into the sky breaking up like matchstick toys as hurricanes hit the southern hemisphere. The world was plunged into a state of extreme emergency, whilst Presidents, Prime ministers, Kings and Queens of the nations turned to every source known to them to fight for their lives and the security of their public.

Still under the impression that the planet was under alien attack, secret missiles were launched and all government headquarters were put on war alert. National security communications crumbled, leaving government bases totally cut off causing widespread panic. The first sightings of the demons across Europe had already had catastrophic effects, as the Sheelka swamped cities, towns and villages collecting souls for their master's army.

CHAPTER FOURTEEN

———⋄◦⋄———

Back in the attic of the inn, the small group huddled together in the candlelight, listening intently for any sound from the street below them.

"They're gone." whispered Jan.

"I wouldn't be too sure about that." said Dougie.

Gerry suddenly dashed across the room and climbed up onto the alcove of the window, pressing his face against the cold glass as he tried to see out onto the street below.

"It's no good;" he said, "all I can see is the snow piled high on the slope of the roof, I can't even make out the street."

"Best come back and sit down, it might be wise to give it another half hour or so." said Mike.

Gerry paced the floor, running his hand through his hair. "I can't just sit here while my wife and child are in that hospital; God only knows what the hells going on there."

Without saying any more, he grabbed up his jacket from the small sofa and put it on.

"What the hell are you doing?" asked Mike, as he quickly joined him by the sofa.

"I can't sit here wondering and hoping and bloody praying while Mia and Alison are in that building where all manner of strange things have been going on."

Mike put his hands on his friend's shoulders. "Listen to me, Gerry ... you'll get yourself killed wading through six feet of snow with god knows what is lurking under it. At least wait until daylight and then we'll all go, maybe by then we'll have a better idea of what the streets are like ... "

"Quiet!" Dougie held his hand up, silencing the men.

Everyone in the room froze like cold marble statues, their breaths held, and the icy tingle of fear winding its way up their spines, numbing their brains. On the other side of the door they heard footsteps, slowly ascending the stairs.

Jan covered her mouth with one hand whilst she grabbed hold of Kate's arm with the other. The men moved into the centre of the room, Mike stood poised with a crowbar that he had spied lying against a free standing cupboard earlier, whilst Dougie grabbed a pot of boiling water from the calor gas stove. Gerry grabbed a heavy brass candle stick that had been sitting on an occasional table near the sofa.

They waited … for what seemed an endless time before the door was burst open. In the scuffle that followed the women screamed, and the men wielded their weapons around, wildly stabbing and thrusting them in mid-air as total chaos broke out.

The room was suddenly filled with flashlights and a voice screamed out orders to "stand down!" … the same voice then ordered everyone to drop their weapons, and stand against the wall with their hands on their heads. Everyone complied, and they waited whilst the rest of the room was searched. One black clad guy cracked a cylinder strip onto the table and the room lit up like a Christmas tree. As their eyes adjusted to the light, they saw that they were surrounded by solders dressed in black from head to toe and each had rifles pointed at them.

The one who stood in the middle of the semi-circle introduced himself as Sergeant William Smith SAS; "One of you will answer my questions, and the rest of you don't move a muscle."

After ten minutes of questions and answers, the squad sergeant ordered his men to stand down, and everyone else, with the exception of Gerry, was told to sit at the table.

Sergeant Smith led Gerry to the far end of the room and spoke quietly to him; "There are at least forty dead people lying outside the premises and by the look of the tracks in the snow they came from here, so what happened?"

"I was hoping you were here to tell us that;" said Gerry, adding "surely you must know what the hell's killing people?"

The sergeant looked uncomfortable as his eyes searched Gerry's face; "No, not exactly," he said "but these things are not aliens from outer space, if you want my opinion … they're out of hell."

Gerry slumped down on a small chair that sat in the corner of the room and ran his hand through his hair.

Smith leaned one hand on the wall and moved in closer; "I suspected that you knew something about what's going on here, and I suggest you tell me." He knelt down so that he was on eye level with Gerry. "I came this close to one of those mother fuckers;" he said, leaning closer still until Gerry's vision became blurred, "and these babies don't mess around, their fucking flesh and blood killing machines. Now I've seen some bad bastards in my time but these things beat me, brother."

Gerry suddenly shot up from his seat and was immediately surrounded by SAS soldiers pointing guns at him.

"Easy men." said Smith, who made a sign to one of his men telling him to get on the other side of Gerry. The soldier moved to the opposite side of his sergeant.

"Look I know this sounds ridiculous;" said Gerry, "but this all started at the city hospital. There's some sort of paranormal phenomenon going on there and not only that, my wife and child are there."

The sergeant and his men looked at Gerry in complete confusion.

"What the hell are you talking about man?" said the sergeant.

"For God's sake listen to him!" shouted Mike, from his position at the table, "He's right, it is that damn place!"

"Talk, and talk fast." said Smith.

Gerry explained about the emails, the accidents, miraculous recoveries, and the child Wendy who claimed to see angels, his daughter's claim that an angel walked by the side of his wife's stretcher the night of the accident and Shaun's disappearance.

"That night, all our lives changed, and no matter what happens next, I'm going to the hospital to be with my wife and child."

One of the squad on the other side of the room said, "Sarge, didn't we get a mayday from that place?"

Smith answered, "Yeah, but McCoon's squad took it."

"We haven't heard anything back sir!"

"Move out!" the sergeant ordered. "Sloan and Walsh, take charge of the civilians."

In less than fifteen minutes Mike, Jan and Gerry were heading up the fire escape stairs on the outside of a building opposite the guest house that led to a flat roof where a chopper waited. Dougie and his family opted to stay behind.

CHAPTER FIFTEEN

The demons in hell were rejoicing as they watched Andy's soul transform. The more powerful he became, the more evil his appearance and soon he would be fully converted into one of hell's own demons.

Shaun had been taken through Gohan, and placed into an even darker domain where all he could see was a stone slab that stood beneath a huge slate arch. It was almost time for him to be joined by the protectors of hell, Andy and Satan himself. Only then would the killing of the boy take place, and it would be Andy's initiation into Satan's kingdom.

The terrified boy sat on cold slabs, his knees bent close to his chest with his arms folded tightly around them as he swayed gently back and forth whilst softly praying to God and all his angels, to save him from this torment.

From out of the gloom, a small gnarled figure shuffled toward him, its grotesque face bright with anticipation. Its head appeared to have no neck structure attached to it and it seemed to have been an afterthought, stuck onto the twisted body.

"It's a bit late for prayers, boy." it said. "Who do you think is going to listen to you?" It was so close now that Shaun could smell its rancid breath and as it shuffled even closer, the boy let out a scream. Its eyes flashed deep green as it laughed at the fear that crossed the boy's face.

It raised a knotted finger to its lips; "Oh dear, I think I may have offended you?" it said sardonically. "Oh you poor thing, and here I am trying to make you feel right at home." Its laugh rang out so loudly that Shaun thought his eardrums would burst!

"Do you know what I'm going to do, boy? I'm going to tell you the story of your life, and if you think you feel bad now, just wait until I am finished!" Its laugh roared out once more and Shaun suddenly sprang to his feet and ran head down towards the creature. Grabbing hold of its arms he kicked out at its twisted body, all the while screaming so that he could drown out the sound of its laughter.

Finally, it threw the boy off; with flashes of anger sweeping over its face it ran at Shaun, but stopped short before impact, and to its utter surprise the boy did not cower.

"Feeling very brave all of a sudden, are we? Well you won't feel like that for much longer; especially when you are tied down on that slab over there whilst you're little human body is torn to shreds! Oh how you will scream and squirm."

"No!" Shaun screamed, "leave me alone."

"My dear child, I have no intentions of leaving you alone; that would never do now, would it? It is my job to make sure that you know exactly who you are; or I should say who you were. You have roamed the earth for one thousand years, enjoying all its pleasantries, think about it;" it said, pausing in reflection; "it seems so unfair that all that life was given to you. You, who became stronger and more powerful with every life cycle, planning and plotting against us with him at your side." he pointed upwards. "By him; I mean your God. Your God named you Reathak which means Earth Walker. It was his intention to send you earthbound to parents of your own choosing time and time again so that you would finally become immortal. Each time you married you chose the same wife and together you had offspring that automatically became immortal angels, running around earth trying to make it a better place. Well as you can understand, we can't let this go on; not if we are to survive here in hell. It has been one thousand years since your creation and in two hours from now that time will have elapsed, which means you and the one they call Wendy; or to use her proper title Theannar which means Heaven's Tear will die here in Hell's own glory. Well I'm glad we had this little chat; we like to keep our residents up to date." said the creature as it turned to leave.

"Who are you?" asked Shaun … it turned around to face the boy once again.

"Who am I?" The creature spread its arms out from the sides of its distorted body and laughed once again, only this time the sound blasting from its throat was even more menacing than before. As the boy watched, the creature's appearance slowly changed into one of human form which was more terrifying than its previous one, for this man was the one who dominated Shaun's nightmares. Ever since his first memories this man had haunted his dreams; dreams that no child should suffer. As he gazed at the face he knew so well, his mind took him back through his nightmares to his very first encounter with him. He shuddered as his recollection flickered, like the turning on of a florescent light that lit every corner of his mind. He shook his head and closed his eyes in a vain attempt to rid himself of the images that turned his nights into abject terror.

The man before him laughed softly as he said, "Where is your saviour now, boy? Can you see him?" He turned, putting his forefinger mockingly to his lips; "Oh perhaps we should search for him, I wonder if he could be hiding beneath this rock." He threw his head back and laughed again; louder this time, before he sat on the rock and folded his arms whilst gleefully observing the child's torment.

No matter what Shaun did, his memories flooded through his mind like an ocean and once again, he found himself reliving his first encounter with this terrifying man who sat not five feet away from him. As always his nightmare began the same way with a sudden realisation that he was in complete darkness. Slowly as the blackness became grey and the grey turned into a murky silver colour. He found himself in a maze but instead of hedgerows, this maze was compiled of black brick walls. He waited for the sound of the hooves and the roar of the beast as it came closer; as always, he would run through the twisting passageways frantically searching for a way of escape until he found himself in a dead end frenetically trying to scramble up the black shiny surface of the wall. Exhausted, he stood facing the wall and he knew that it was behind him … waiting for him to turn around. As he turned around the huge black bull waited menacingly at the opposite end of the passageway; its right front leg pawing the ground, its black eyes firmly fixed on him. Its terrifying roar preceded the charge as tons of muscle and flesh headed toward him … and as always, in his dream, just before impact, the bull took on the human form of the man sitting before him.

The terrified boy knew the next words that would be spoken as his mind persistently ran through the dream scene like a movie. The man stood before him and tilted his head slightly to the side as he said, "Are you coming home with me?" The man's laughter filled the air once again as Shaun snapped out of his dream state like a press-stud.

"Leave me alone!" he screamed. "Go away; I hate you!"

Observing the boy closely, the beast stood up and walked across the small distance that separated them looking like any man off the street; clad in a dark suit, grey shirt and dark tie. His face was not ugly but handsome, and his dark hair was short and neat. Closer still he came and Shaun recoiled as he gazed into his eyes.

"Who am I, Reathak?" he asked once again as he pressed his face closer still so that his nose was almost touching Shaun's. "I am the Devil!"

Chapter Sixteen

———◆———

Back on the children's ward, all the Angels were aware of the changed atmosphere that hung in the air like thick fog. The demons knew that Wendy had been taken from the earth and was receiving her instructions in God's Heaven. The portal would only remain open for one and a half hours; time was running out, and all of Hell's Demons were furious.

Mordrand guarded the entrance to the corridor that led to the ward. No Angel could remain in the basement for a lengthy period for their essence would shine through spotlighting them from the others. The close proximity of the portal would have catastrophic effects on their souls, for they could fight the Demons that prowled over the earth but no Angel could survive Hell's atmosphere.

Wendy could not stay in Heaven for an indefinite period for she must return as a mortal to live out her assigned life span before she and Shaun would fulfil their destiny as earth's immortal protectors.

In Heaven, Shrancanna waited whilst the child received her truth and though she would return as a child she would have the wisdom of an adult.

Although Wendy's body lay in the Dome of Truth, her mind took her through tangible experiences until the present day. The child was to relive her birth, and as she did so the realization of the identity of her earth father became clear; his name was Andy Morrison! She was also aware of his present situation as one of Hell's newest recruits, and of his intention to kill Shaun. She struggled against her deep slumber as the realization of her father's past hit home, but she was soothed by the voice of her mother as she reminded her of her destiny. She knew that her time here had elapsed and as she awakened Shrancanna was by her side.

No words were spoken between the two as she was once again cradled in her daughter's arms before making the journey back to earth. The mother and daughter did not look back as they swiftly retreated lest they would linger.

On the children's ward the little gathering waited patiently for the return of the child who was destined to save the world. In the corridors of the hospital the war between Demons and Angels had begun once more when the realization of Wendy's heavenly visit had become apparent.

In the nurse's office within the ward, the Angels still in hospital uniforms prepared for the arrival of Shrancanna and their mother Wendy. The children still slumbered, unaware of the world's danger, and Mia, Anna and Clare sat together talking.

"If the worst happens and they win," said Clare, "then the whole thing would have been pointless!"

"Sitting here like this makes me want to agree with you," replied Anna "but the real thing that gets me are those emails, I just can't get my head round why they were sent in the first place. They warned us all about the accidents but none of them were prevented and if they were sent from hell, then why?"

Mia, looking thoughtful, tightened the blanket around her shoulders before saying, "If they were sent from hell then perhaps they understand the human element in us more than we ourselves do."

"I don't understand." said Clare.

"Well, when I was a child and my mother forbade me to go to a certain place, it only made me want to go all the more and maybe that's the human element in us that they were counting on."

"But what if we hadn't gone?" asked Clare.

"If we hadn't then I think we would have died in some other way." said Mia.

"But what would have been the point of that?" asked Clare, looking puzzled.

"We would never have had our near death experiences and we would never have understood the connection between us." said Mia.

"The connection between us." said Anna softly. "So you mean that we have been together in circumstances throughout our past lives and somehow no matter what we do, or where we are in the world we will always connect."

"I certainly hope so." said Mia, as she clasped the hands of her friends.

A short time later, from the little glass partitioned office there appeared a golden light that was so intense that the whole of the ward glowed, lighting up every corner of the room and moments later the child was back.

As she walked into the ward, Mia and her friends were struck by the change in the child's demeanour. She was only four years old but there was an assurance about her that was steadfast.

Out in the corridors the battle raged on and Mia prayed that the invisible screen across the door to the ward would hold. Wendy and her Angels wasted no time in preparing to leave the ward and enter the floor above where Andy's human form lay deep in his coma.

Mordrand flew along the corridor toward the basement to create a distraction that would give the others a few more precious minutes. The portal, in the floor of the darkest corner of the basement, looked as though it was a section of ocean for its colour was sea green and there was a mist swirling over its turbulent surface. The demons caught sight of Mordrand and screamed like Banshees as they flew toward him. His allies from other areas of the hospital, some in nurse's uniforms and others clad in dressing gowns, soared on pure white wings down through the corridors to face the demons of hell.

On the upper floor the perilous journey had begun. Shrancanna, carrying the child who was wrapped in a blanket, was surrounded by her brothers and sisters as they quietly inched their way up the darkened stairway that led to Andy's room. Unable to fly for their essence would fill the air and alert the demons, they held their breath, as each step seemed to take a lifetime.

CHAPTER SEVENTEEN

———◆———

In the whiteout high above the hospital, the pilot struggled to keep the chopper on course. Conditions were so fierce that he was unable to stabilize the machine as it rotated wildly in the furious sky.

"Jesus Christ man, we're going to crash!" shouted one of the men as they spun helplessly. There was no time for any other comments as the machine suddenly turned sideways heading straight for the ground below. As it was, the pilot had only overrun the landing strip by ten yards. The rota blades churned up the snow that was piled high on the ground like whipped cream before they finally shattered; sending shards of steel flying back up into the air like ping-pong balls. The sound of glass shattering and metal crunching rang through the still darkness like the scream of a murder victim. When it was over the only other sound to be heard was the whine of the dying engine.

Inside the hospital the battle raged with greater fury than before, and time was perilously close to the closing of the portal. Throughout the corridors of hell, all manner of demons raged their fury for only one hour remained till world domination; but only if the girl was brought through the doorway to hell before midnight

In the children's ward the evil forces could not break through the invisible barrier that sealed the door; instead, the cots levitated and hung eerily in the air. The tables and chairs rattled and jumped across the floor as though they were dancing to some unheard Satanic melody.

Mia screamed as she tried to hold onto the leg of Alison's bed but it was no use, as it swayed around in the air she lost her grip and fell to the ground. She screamed and was helped to her feet by one of the Angels wearing a nurse's uniform.

"You must remain strong;" she said "for fear will attract the demons. Recall your visit to The Kingdom of Heaven and know that he will never desert you. Your mission is upon you child, trust in the one who created you." As the Angel's voice faded away like a dying melody, Mia's vision altered and she could see beyond the hospital walls to the wreckage that held her husband, her friends and the military crew.

She turned to Anna and Clare and before she was able to speak, they both told her that they too had seen the wreckage. Calmly, and with no words passing between them, all three women walked to the farthest corner of the ward and opened a door that led them out onto a fire escape landing that was waist deep in snow. They headed down the metal stairs so swiftly that they wondered at the ease with which they made their descent, and as they glided through the thick snow they did not feel the icy cold.

Lying among the twisted wreckage, Sergeant Smith tried to move away from the metal bar that dug into his back, when he realised that both his arms were broken. He could hear a soft moan near him somewhere to his right and it took him a few seconds to realise that Jan was still alive.

"Can you hear me, Mrs Pierce? Are you okay, can you move?" Jan tried to move toward the Sergeant but she was too weak to force her way through the rubble.

"I can't move;" she called, "something's pinning me down!"

"Okay, don't try, just lie still and I'll come to you, you're going to be all right, do you hear me?"

He dug his heels into a metal grid that lay in front of him; beads of sweat popped like blisters on his forehead as he tried to inch himself forward. He cried out in pain as he hurled himself forward so that he was in a lying position, and with his arms pinned to his side he rolled over. He couldn't breathe without excruciating pain and he realised that his ribs were also broken. He lay in the wreckage, exhausted from his effort but determined to stay alive he rolled again but could only get half way round as the pain threatened to render him unconscious. For a short time he lay looking out onto the snow and longed for its icy cold touch over his body. Suddenly he saw lights in the distance; he blinked his eyes several times, afraid that he was seeing things, or worse … was close to death. His mind was racing as he tried to distinguish what type of vehicle it could be that could glide seemingly effortlessly through such deep snow. He closed his eyes and tried to regulate his breathing; his pain no longer localised but consuming his entire body.

"God help us." he softly called as he opened his eyes. His vision was blurred and he blinked several times before he realised that three women were gliding through the snow toward the wreckage. The light that he had seen earlier was surrounding these women like very bright auras around every part of them.

"Oh my God," he whispered; "you're Angels!"

Clare smiled at the dying man as she laid her hand on his chest; "It's not your time yet, you have too much to do here." As he stared wide-eyed at this young woman he could feel the pain from his broken body disintegrate until finally it was no more; then a surge of pure energy flowed through him and in that instant, he knew that it was life itself returning to his broken body. Still wide-eyed the Sergeant sat up, unable to take his eyes from this woman who had restored his life and unashamed tears ran from his eyes like huge clear crystals.

"Quickly now;" said Clare as she moved on to the next crew member "we must get away from here as soon as possible."

Jumping up, Sergeant Smith immediately started to clear away the debris to make way for the other miracles. Mia kissed her husband and grabbed hold of his hand as she urged him to get to his feet; and like the others in the tangled helicopter he too was wide-eyed as they set off; and to the astonishment of them all the path that the women had taken lay bare of snow.

Back in the bowels of hell, Andy's form had become so grotesque that no trace of humanity was left. Surrounded by malevolent beasts he made his way to the pit of Gohan in order to mutilate the chosen child upon the dark altar that had been the silent bloody witness to many ritual slayings.

The Keepers laughed with glee and anticipation at the thought of the upcoming slaughter that would secure their wicked existence for ever more.

Shaun cowered from the half human, half beast that now stood before him.

"You cannot escape little human." said the beast as it smiled widely.

"Get away from me!" the terrified boy screamed as he ran blindly in total panic. The evil laughter of all who were now gathered in the pit rang out menacingly as each way the boy turned he was caught by the hideous creatures, and tossed back into the centre of the pit.

"Ha." laughed the Kassad that had previously spoken to the boy as it now stood in front of him once again with its hands held up in front of its chest wickedly tapping its fingers together in malicious glee. "How the mortal fears; look at his terror!" it drooled. "And the wonderful thing about it is that he has not even begun to experience it!" There followed a frenzied excitement throughout the stench filled pit as the beasts rejoiced.

As Andy walked along hell's corridors, his strength multiplying with every step, the sights that had once been so terrifying now delighted him as he became aware of the beauty of evil. He thought of the boy praying earlier, and of his own reluctance to let himself be seen as he turned into one of the monsters the child had been so afraid of. He roared like a bull at the very thought and quickened his step toward the pit. He was eager to show the boy just how much of a monster he really was now, as a fully fledged member of the Sheelka.

Back in the hospital Wendy and her Angels had finally reached the floor that held Andy's human form, and just as they reached the door of his room they heard a guttural laugh behind them. Shrancanna swiftly turned around to face the Angel whose heart was as black as coal.

"Zeenkell!" she cried, as she passed the child to Asha who darted into the room along with the other protectors leaving her alone with their old enemy.

"How you disappoint me;" he told her, "and here was I thinking that you and your little hoard would have come up with a better plan than this!" he spread out his arms and laughed. "Do you think that letting her see her father will save her life? How uninspiring. However, you have done me the greatest of favours by moving her from the protection of the children's ward. And now," he said contemptuously "I believe she is mine."

As he moved toward the door, Shrancanna thrust her arms out, creating a barrier between them. His eyes flashed deep red as his anger exploded like a time bomb; and grabbing her by the throat he tossed her aside like a rag doll.

"Get out of my way bitch!" he screamed, as Shrancanna was propelled along the corridor. On her wings she flew back to the door in an instant and was once again facing Zeenkell. He hissed into her face like an angry tiger as she thrust her fist into his upper abdomen just below his rib cage. He screamed in pain as her fingers curled around his small intestine; she plunged deeper all the while moving him backwards away from the door.

"This child will not die in hell, demon," she said, "and when her mission is complete all captured souls in your domain will rise up and return to their father in the Kingdom of Heaven leaving hell's soul basin empty; and the likes of you will be lost forevermore."

Unable to move, Zeenkell threw his head back onto his shoulders and screamed in agony as her essence burned the inside of his body. Finally he fell backwards leaving her free of his filthy innards; and seconds later, just as though she had pulled on a glove his filth melted away from her hand and forearm.

As he squirmed on the floor he heard the door of Andy's room close; and as he opened his eyes he saw Mordrand standing over him. Suddenly there was an explosion from the direction of the clinical laboratory area and Mordrand was propelled along the full length of the corridor. The huge ball of fire rumbled along the passageway like a flaming rock and as Mordrand glanced back Zeenkell had vanished!

Wendy gazed at her father's pale face, and all the angels present stood in a circle around the bed so close to each other that their wings were touching. Once Shrancanna positioned herself by the side of the child, she gently rested her hand on Wendy's shoulder and silently prayed. The atmosphere in the room was so intense that all in attendance felt that if anyone were to move suddenly; the air itself would shatter like glass. Wendy's heart was pounding as she laid her hand upon her father's forehead.

In hell, Andy had reached the pit of Gohan; and just as he entered he was aware of a very different atmosphere drenching the pit like heavy rain. Satan himself stood beneath the portal that's dark surface rolled like angry clouds suspended at the apex of the arched cavity in the dome-like structure that was hell's darkest place.

Satan was physically lifting huge Sheelka soldiers and tossing them through the portal with a strength that belied his human stature.

"Get the bitch!" he screamed, as he threw more members of his deadly army up into the air and through the doorway from hell. "Idiots!" he screamed, as all around him scurried about in complete panic. "There are fifteen minutes left until the portal closes for another thousand years and my so called flawless army can't bring a child from there," he pointed to the portal, "to here! It would seem that all I have taught you has been in vain."

His face transformed into one of pure evil as his eyes became pools of fire. "If she is not here within the next few minutes you will pay for all eternity as I toss your souls into the bowl of torment." Suddenly he threw his head back onto his shoulders and howled like a tormented wolf before he leapt into the air and disappeared through the portal.

Hearts of angels stood still as he emerged into the corridor of the basement and they were forced to look upon him stripped of his disguise. For he was the horned beast that held so many terrors for man and immortal; here was the beast that defiled every man, woman and child and haunted their dreams; brought down nations upon the war torn world. Here he stood with all the power of destruction at his command; he grinned exultantly at his audience facing him in an ordinary corridor of an ordinary hospital basement.

From the centre of the angels emerged Mordrand who walked along the middle of the corridor until he stopped in front of the beast. Satan laughed; and its rasping sound echoed throughout the entire building.

"Ah, little Mordrand," he said as his eyes glowed with anticipation; "Your saviour's little message boy, and what do you think you are going to do? Save the world? Save the child? What a fool you are angel." he said mockingly; then with one sweep of his arm he sent Mordrand crashing backwards with such force that he was thrown along the entire length of the corridor, smashing into the wall at the far end leaving the imprint of his body on the brickwork. The next second the beast vanished, leaving nothing behind except his stench.

Chapter Eighteen

In Hell, Andy stood over the black marble slab where Shaun lay tied down and terrified, waiting for the blow that would stop his heart. Through his fear he became aware of a change in the monster lingering over him as he suddenly started to shake his head violently as though shaking off a bad memory.

In his head, Andy could see the face of Wendy bending over his body that lay in the hospital room. Her lips were close to his ear as she told him that it was his own daughter who together with Shaun was destined to save the world. He screamed in protest as he clasped his hands over his ears in a futile effort to block out her words. The child on the slab suddenly stopped struggling against his restraints and looked on in amazement as the monster beside him started to physically change into human form.

As his black eyes cleared and transformed into clear blue, he looked down on the child as though he were seeing him for the first time. Shaun became aware of a light surrounding the man and knew that whatever had happened to him; he was no longer the evil monster that had been poised to kill him only moments earlier.

In his hospital room Wendy became aware of a very different atmosphere hanging in the air like a heavy cloud; slowly she looked around the room and saw her angels frozen in time, and turned to stone. Her breathing became fast and shallow as she became aware of his breath on the back of her neck, and the unmistakable stench of the beast himself; and as she slowly turned around and looked into his eyes they were dancing with triumph.

Suddenly grabbing hold of her by the hair he pulled her head back and drew his face close to hers as he whispered, "It's all over now, bitch!" His laugh disgusted her, as she tried to twist her head away from the stench of his breath, but he held her fast. "It's time for you to come home with me, oh it won't be so terrible once you get used to it, in fact you might rather enjoy it." Once again his laugh reverberated throughout the building. When he suddenly swept her up into his arms, she felt as though her ribs were being crushed by his force; and then mercifully she was surrounded in darkness as her body became limp in his grasp.

In hell, Andy's transition was complete; and as he looked down on the boy lying on the slab, tears sprang from his eyes as he released the child and gathered him into his arms.

A few Sheelka soldiers looking on were amazed to see that their latest recruit had somehow managed to slip back into his human form; and suddenly, as realisation of what had transpired hit them they flew to the slab at the altar.

Andy swiftly ran with the boy to the side of the dome where the portal hung like turbulent clouds swirling in the air. He jumped onto a rock in readiness to propel himself up as high as he could and through the portal, when his legs were caught by one of the Sheelka. With all his might he threw the boy upwards and the darkness of the portal became momentarily white as Shaun slipped through it into the world beyond.

The Sheelka pulled Andy back and threw him across the marble slab, and as they swooped down on him he grabbed hold of the sacrificial stiletto and the Sheelka immediately backed off. With fear in their eyes they slowly moved backwards, for this was the only blade that could kill them.

With time running out and the portal growing smaller, Andy ran through the dome with the echo of the whaling of tormented souls as he finally leapt up and into the portal. As he spun through the darkness that slowly lightened to grey he was aware of another body in the tunnel-like structure spinning toward him. As it got closer, he realised that it was the creator of hell and he was carrying his daughter. Still clutching the blade he raised it in readiness to plunge it into the heart of the beast, and as they moved closer, Satan's eyes caught the glint of the blade shining in the grey hue. Suddenly he threw the child off to divert Andy from plunging the knife into his heart and Andy caught his child in his arms he dropped the weapon that sailed downwards to the hellish world that it had come from. As the beast passed him he screamed like a tormented animal as he was propelled back into his domain crushed by his defeat.

By the time Andy's head emerged from the portal it had all but closed and they had to be dragged from its clutches by eager helping hands. There was a silence that surrounded the building like a warm soothing mist that preceded the sunrise as the realisation that the war was over sank in.

As Wendy awoke she looked into the blue eyes of her father that were so much like her own, and as he held her tightly in his arms they wept together. Shaun had been sitting dazed by the side of a doorway looking on; and as he made to move closer to Wendy and her father, the door by his side clicked. He became still as he watched the door slowly open and once again he felt fear creep around his spine as the door was thrust open. His heart missed a beat and his eyes widened as he looked upon the face of his mother who was closely followed by his father, Mia, Gerry and Alison. A troop of soldiers came tumbling out and behind them appeared Clare and Anna.

In Andy's room all that was left of the body that had been in the coma were ashes, spread out on the crumpled bed. The stone that had transfixed the Angels slowly began

211

to crumble away leaving them free once again. From the dark bowels of hell there appeared a light that spread like massive arms, which scooped the captured souls from the bowl of torment; and the tiny glowing orbs became part of the light until every man, woman and child were free, leaving Satan and his Sheelka once more in darkness.

THREE YEARS LATER

It had taken a great deal of time for the world to recover from 'the war' as people referred to it, as indeed it was. For many months following; stories of personal accounts were spread across every front page tabloid. But like all things in life, the stories and sightings of dark winged beings flying through the night sky slowly faded into the past as the world got on with living in the here and now.

It was a mid-summer's day, and the final preparations for the party had been completed. The garden was filled with tables that were draped with pale blue covers, the music system was ready and the food prepared. There were fifty pale blue balloons tied to the back of numerous chairs that sat by the tables; each one with the message that read 'Happy First Wedding Anniversary'.

Andy, Moira and Wendy surveyed the scene with a good measure of satisfaction and were ready for their guests to arrive. The house phone rang out and Andy went inside to answer the call whilst Wendy and her mother did a little bit of tweaking to the already perfect table settings. Moments later he reappeared to let them know that John from the unit had called to say that the boys were on their way.

Since Andy's experience in the corridors of hell, he had changed beyond recognition and instead of dealing drugs he had opened a shelter for kids that were trapped in their addictions. Working closely with the police, he took these kids under his wing and set them onto a twelve step programme of recovery and even helped them find jobs once they were clean and sober. Life was good for the one time bad guy who found his soul again in the depths of hell; and one year ago he had married Wendy's mother.

Wendy and Shaun had become inseparable since the night of Mia's car crash and although they had no memory of the whole experience; they knew instinctively that their paths were intertwined for ever more.

It seemed the guests arrived all at once, and as usual whenever in each other's company Shaun and Wendy huddled in a corner of the garden away from the others happily laughing and talking together.

Anna who also worked at the shelter was happy to let Andy know that their latest recruit was her friend

Clare, who would be working in the financial funding department.

Gerry, Mia, Alison and their new puppy Mazy arrived, who was so excited by the smell of the food that her tail was doing an impressive impersonation of a propeller.

Mike and Sue, who had been laughing at the antics of the young dog, sat down beside them happily enjoying the atmosphere. The Sutherlands, along with their son Jack arrived laden with gifts. The bond between these people was unbreakable and once the party took off the laughter was genuine and the love between them sincere.

It was around seven thirty that evening when one of the boys from the shelter persuaded two others to leave the party and visit a new café named 'Fire and Ice' that had opened in the centre of town.

"This place is brilliant!" exclaimed the excited boy.

"So what's so brilliant about the place?" asked one of the others.

"You go in right; and there's this really weird guy that runs the place; all dressed in black and he wears a vampire like cloak; I'm telling you man this bloke is wicked!. He asks you what your pleasure is right; and then tells you that anything you desire awaits you down in the basement of the café."

"Oh yeah, and what's down in the basement?" asked one of the boys.

"Well, I didn't have time that day to look ... " The boys roared with laughter!

"Skinner's too frightened to go down to the spooky guy's basement. Ha!"

"It's not like that," he insisted. "I had to get back for the N A meeting; you know how Andy hates us to be late and the bloke has been good to us; it's the least we can do to turn up on time."

"Yeah okay; so you want us to go down to the basement with you, is that it?"

"Yeah why not; I saw a kid coming out and he said 'that it was the best experience he had ever had and this kid's been around the world man! He told me that down there, right, were things like holograms right in front of you and you could be in any situation that you like. No daft helmets wired up man, nothing like that; he said 'it's like living on another planet' and all you have to do is think about something and bang! It's right there man."

The boys looked at one another for a moment then unanimously decided to go take a look at this new place.

"Okay wait here." said Skinner "I'll go and tell the chief we're off."

Five minutes after the boys left; Andy felt a sudden uneasiness settle over him but soon shrugged it off, reminding himself that the boys were working their programme and he had to trust them.

Twenty minutes later the boys arrived at Fire and Ice.

"What the hell is this?" laughed one of the boys; "the new big fancy cafe that is nothing but an old black door with a flashing sign above it; gee I can't wait to get in there!" he said sarcastically.

"Shut it Pimples," said Skinner. "I'm telling you this place is like another world, just get in the fucking door and you'll see."

As they opened the door and stepped inside they were utterly amazed at the size of the place. At the far end stood a large fully equipped bar that was illuminated in purple and green lights. In front of that were tables arranged around a large music system which had flashing lights above it. On the adjoining wall sat a row of computers where kids sat playing games, whilst others played on pinball machines. Behind them was an alcove which had a strange yellow light inside which was almost murky, making it difficult to see into the area from where they were standing and above it was a sign that read 'EMAILS FROM HELL'.

"What the hell does that mean?" said one of the boys.

"One of those new games that Skinner was banging on about." said Pimples.

"Oh it's no game." said one of the guys who was seated at a table nearby.

"What do you mean mate?" asked Skinner.

"Well;" said the young guy as he stood up and walked over to where they were standing; "that is the room where emails with a slightly menacing touch are sent."

"What kind of emails?"

"Well, imagine that you were sent a message telling you that you were going to die! What would you do?"

"Tell whoever sent it to fuck off." said Skinner.

The guy laughed as he returned to the table where he sat down again before saying, "That's what I thought you'd say; human beings are prone to ignoring warning signs but, even when they do, they cannot escape fate. No; the emails are designed to frighten the holy shit out of them before the inevitable happens."

The boys looked at each other before Skinner said, "Come on. we're getting the fuck out of this joint." As they made their way to the door they heard a rustling noise and as they turned to see where it came from … sure enough 'the weird guy' appeared through a black beaded curtain from the left of the room.

"Good evening gentlemen," he said, "what will be your pleasure tonight?"

"We want to go down to the basement; how much is it?" asked Skinner.

"As much as you want to pay!" answered 'the weird guy'.

"Yeah, well that ain't much of an answer."

"Trust me; you will understand once you have a few … shall we say encounters?" he said as he led the way down the stairs.

The boys felt slightly nervous as they descended the narrow stairway and for no other reason than to have something to say, Skinner said, "What's your name mate?" The weird guy stopped at the foot of the stairs and turned to look at the boys before saying, "I go by many names, but you can call me Zeenkell!"

The End

ABOUT THE AUTHOR

Diane Marshall was born in a tenement flat in Johnstone, Renfrewshire in July 1951. For many years she wrote short stories which she kept in a secret place until 2001 when she finally compiled them into a book of short stories; following that she wrote a play called 'The Attendants' which was staged in The Mitchell Theatre, Glasgow; had an all star cast, and became a tremendous hit with theatre goers. Hailed as 'One of the finest writing talents to emerge in Scotland for years.' The Scotsman, August 2003, Mrs Marshall has now completed her first novel 'Beyond The Light', a fictional story about near death experience Mrs Marshall lives with her husband near Lesmahagow Lanark.